EPHESIA GRAMMATA:
ANCIENT HISTORY
AND
MODERN PRACTICE

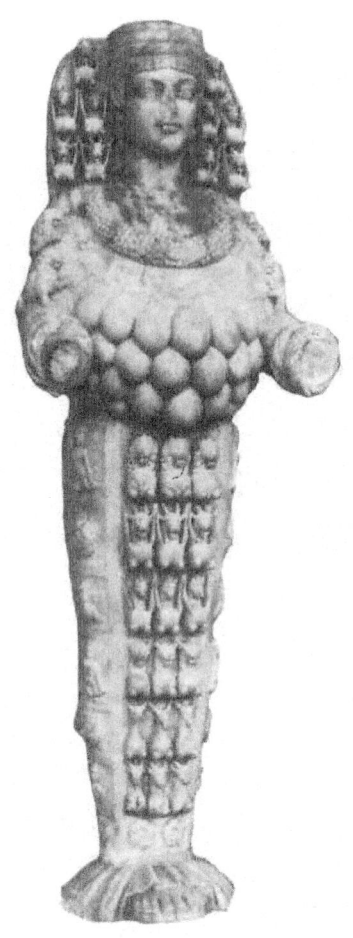

ii

EPHESIA GRAMMATA: ANCIENT HISTORY AND MODERN PRACTICE

P. Sufenas Virius Lupus

The Red Lotus Library

July, 2014

Unless otherwise specified, the illustrations in this book are public domain photographs obtained from the website http://www.antinoos.info/.

The Red Lotus Library is the publication imprint of the Ekklesía Antínoou, a queer, Graeco-Roman-Egyptian syncretist reconstructionist polytheist group dedicated to Antinous, the deified lover of the Roman Emperor Hadrian, and related divine figures.

The Red Lotus Library
Anacortes, WA, U.S.A.

Copyright © 2014 by P. Sufenas Virius Lupus

All rights reserved. No written part of the present book may be reproduced by any means or in any form without express permission from the author, except for brief quotations embedded within literary or scholarly articles or reviews.

Printed by CreateSpace in the United States of America

Table of Contents

Preface and Acknowledgments   vii
Artemis of Ephesus   1

ASKION, KATASKION:
    "Shadowless, Shadowy"–
    A Brief History of the Ephesia
    Grammata   3
LIX, TETRAX:
    "Earth, Seasons"–
    Examples of the Ephesia Grammata
    in Ancient Texts   26
DAMNAMANEUS:
    "Sun"–
    The Ephesia Grammata as
    Protective Amulets   48
AISIA:
    "True Word/Voice"–
    The Ephesia Grammata as
    Divine Grammatical Beings   66
ENDASION:
    "Kindling Hairy Distributors (?!?)"–
    The Ephesia Grammata as
    Divinatory System   87

which this survey is based are diffuse and highly variable in nature. The one short published study that has been done solely on the subject of the Ephesia Grammata—that of Carl Wessely in *Ephesia Grammataaus Papyrusrollen, Inschriften, Gemmen etc.*(Vienna: A. Pichlers Witwe & Sohn, 1886)—is short (only 38 pages), quite outdated, and in German, though now easily available in a low-quality reprint. Little that is in it cannot be found elsewhere, in more up-to-date resources in English, which have been relied upon to a very large extent in what follows below.

After having worked with the Ephesia Grammata for more than two years of (at least) daily practice, and experiencing their integration into the fuller context of my spiritual life and work, I feel that it is time to share this knowledge with the wider polytheist public, as well as anyone who might be interested otherwise. The system works best when it is worked with on a constant, dedicated, and regular basis. Experience is one of the best teachers on this matter, as so many others.

The present volume would not be possible without the contributions, support, and input of a wide variety of individuals. In particular, I would like to recognize the twenty-ish attendees at my PantheaCon 2014 presentation (including Brandy Williams, Ted Gill, Tony Mierzwicki, JoAnn Mierzwicki, Jeremy Glick, and Tristissima et alia laughing and weeping) for providing the first public outlet and very valuable feedback on my initial sharing of this information; Galina Krasskova and Sannion for hosting the Polytheist Leadership Conference in July of 2014, where this information was shared again with the public and the present volume was launched; Theanos Thrax (the Anomalous Thracian) for his sage advice and often divinatory insight; my students Tara Cottrill and Becca Honeycutt for bringing their own brand of influence (often in the form of automobile transportation and pleasant lunches) to this text; Duffi McDermott for providing material and moral support during the process of writing (and far beyond it!); my mother and my sister for providing (respectively) a place to write this book and the cover for it; Michael Sebastian Lvx for producing the image of the Tetrad++

Group's sigil that adorns the back of this book; and, most importantly, the deities and other divine beings I devotedly serve, among them the Tetrad++ Group (especially Paneros), the Trophimoi of Herodes Attikos (and especially Polydeukion), the Divine Hadrian and the Divine Sabina, the Divine Matidia, Glykon, Chnoubis, Palaimon/Melikertes, Thoth, Wepwawet, Hermanubis, Ianus, Hermes, Hekate, Cú Chulainn, Finn mac Cumhaill, Lucius Marius Vitalis, the hero son of Eos Memnon of the Ethiopians, Bes, Hathor, Hanuman, Durga, and Kali (the three of whom were especially involved in the last weeks of this book's production), Disciplina, Artemis of Ephesus (whose true name is Upis), the Ephesia Grammata themselves (and particularly *DAMNAMENEUS*), and of course Antinous of Bithynia—about whom on this occasion I will say, as a variation on our usual ritual acclamation: *Hic est unde, Hic est unde, Hic est unde vita venit!* I dedicate this effort to them and their glory!

—P. Sufenas Virius Lupus
Anacortes, WA, U.S.A.
July, 2014

Artemis of Ephesus

Fallen from the heavens, shadowless,
and kept in the temple, shadowy,
the sacred image, wood not from earth,
persisted across changing seasons
and the rising and setting of sun,
protected by the magic of word.

ASKION the first of holy word,
its meaning said by priests, "shadowless,"
the Megabyzoi, by light of sun
with gold-inscribed wood, lines shadowy
predict the turning of life's seasons
and protect mortals upon the earth.

Second letter of strength on round earth,
the power of uncertainty's word
amidst the shifting warmth of seasons
and full moon's face, bright and shadowless,
is KATASKION, or "shadowy,"
the condition of life under sun.

The greatest object beneath the sun
is the third word, LIX, the fertile "earth,"
teeming with life in nooks shadowy,
affirmation of matter in word;
and the fourth, TETRAX, doubt shadowless,
is change and time, for it means "seasons."

DAMNAMANEUS, worldly seasons,
is the passing overhead of "sun,"
erasing all worries, shadowless,
scattering clouds over the fair earth;
and AISIA, the sixth, is true "word,"
though in meaning it is shadowy.

Her persistence is not shadowy,
lasting throughout trials of past seasons
and marauding followers of Word
born at the time of Unconquered Sun—
Artemis of Ephesus, all earth
sings her praises, faultless, shadowless!

Fame not shadowy, brighter than sun,
triumphant seasons upon the earth—
great goddess' word, virtue shadowless!

ASKION, KATASKION:

"Shadowless, Shadowy"

A Brief History of the Ephesia Grammata

THE Ephesia Grammata, or "Ephesian Letters," were one of the most popular and well-known short magical formulas known in the ancient world.[1] The uses of the Ephesia Grammata are diverse, and will be treated in the subsequent chapters. Here, an attempt will be made at a brief history of the Ephesia Grammata and some of the figures associated with them.

---

[1] Translations of many of the ancient texts concerned with the Ephesia Grammata can be found at a webpage called "Healing and Protection" from Bryn Mawr College: http://www.brynmawr.edu/classics/redmonds/H5-CSTS212.html. These include passages by Anaxilas (via Athenaeus), Menander, Plutarch, the *Suda*, Eustathius, Photius, Clement of Alexandria, Hesychius, the *Testament of Solomon*, and several magical tablets and *PGM* spells. Subsequent notes will indicate whether texts discussed are available here, if not in other referenced texts.

Ancient Ephesus was heavily associated with magic, and thus the phrase "Ephesian Letters" can mean "magical words" in general,[2] which is what modern scholars of ancient magic refer to as *voces magicae*.[3] While we would do well to be suspicious of the source, The Christian New Testament's *Acts of the Apostles* chapter 19 has an account of Saul of Tarsus (a.k.a. "St." Paul) attempting to make converts in Ephesus, and "A number of those who practiced magic collected their books and burned them publicly; when the value of these books was calculated, it was found to come to fifty thousand silver coins" (19:19).[4] Immediately after this, a riot occurs in which the

---

[2] Georg Luck, *Arcana Mundi: Magic and the Occult in the Greek and Roman Worlds* (Baltimore and London: The Johns Hopkins University Press, 1985), p. 17.

[3] John G. Gager, *Curse Tablets and Binding Spells from the Ancient World* (Oxford and New York: Oxford University Press, 1992), p. 267. *Voces magicae* are often non-Greek-derived words or names, or sometimes strings of vowels or vowel-consonant syllables, found in the spell formulae of Graeco-Egyptian spells, as well as inscribed on curse tablets, amulets, and other objects. Johan August Alm, *Tartaros: On the Orphic and Pythagorean Underworld, and the Pythagorean Pentagram* (Hercules, CA: Three Hands Press, 2013), pp. 142-143, lacks a bit of nuance on the difference between *voces magicae* in general and the canonical six Ephesia Grammata.

[4] New Revised Standard Version.

people of Ephesus shout "Great is Artemis of the Ephesians!" (19:28, 34). In the late second century CE, it seems that in response to a plague that occurred in 165, the oracle of Apollon at Claros suggested that a golden statue of Artemis of Ephesus holding two torches be brought and enshrined as Artemis Soteira ("the Savior") in the unidentified community near Ephesus where this took place, and subsequently that wax images of Artemis of Ephesus also be melted by the torches on the statue at the inaugural festival of the goddess.[5]

The statue of Ephesian Artemis herself was said to be the origin of the Ephesia Grammata, as—via Pausanias the lexicographer—they were engraved on the feet, girdle, and crown of her sacred image in the temple at Ephesus.[6] More will be

---

[5] Fritz Graf, *Magic in the Ancient World*, trans. Franklin Philip (Cambridge: Harvard University Press, 1999), p. 163.

[6] Chester C. McCown, "The Ephesia Grammata in Popular Belief," *Transactions and Proceedings of the American Philological Association* 54 (1923), pp. 128-140 at 129; Richard Gordon, "Imagining Greek and Roman Magic," in Valerie Flint, Richard Gordon, Georg Luck, and Daniel Ogden, *Witchcraft and Magic in Europe, Volume 2: Ancient*

said on the statue of Artemis of Ephesus, and those associated with it, subsequently in the present chapter.

The most common traditional formula for the Ephesia Grammata gives six words as the "letters." These, given in majuscule and minuscule Greek and their Latin transliterations, are:

ΑΣΚΙΟΝ ασκιον
ASKION (or *ASKI*)
ΚΑΤΑΣΚΙΟΝ κατασκιον
KATASKION (or *KATASKI*)
ΛΙΞ λιξ
LIX
ΤΕΤΡΑΞ τετραξ
TETRAX
ΔΑΜΝΑΜΕΝΕΥΣ δαμναμενευς
DAMNAMENEUS
ΑΙΣΙΑ αισια
AISIA (or *AISION*)

Greece and Rome (London: The Athlone Press, 1999), pp. 159-275 at 171-172.

On at least one occasion, there is a seventh letter, **ENDASION**, which will be dealt with in subsequent chapters below. I tend to personally prefer the –*ION* endings for the first two for metrical reasons, whereas the –*IA* ending for the last then makes it a palindrome. Whichever forms of the different letters appeals to you most should be the one used. When pronouncing the Ephesia Grammata, remember that the vowels concerned are the longer, Continental European vowels (as one would find in Latin, and most Continental European languages) rather than the shorter American and British English vowels.

In addition to being called the Ephesia Grammata, this formula is also sometimes referred to as the "*aski kataski* formula,"[7] or in other cases as the "Orphic formula."[8] In light of the latter, the connection between Orphic,

---

[7] Roy Kotansky, "Incantations and Prayers for Salvation on Inscribed Greek Amulets," in Christopher A. Faraone and Dirk Obbink (eds.), *Magika Hiera: Ancient Greek Magic & Religion* (Oxford and New York: Oxford University Press, 1991), pp. 107-137 at 121.

[8] Hans Dieter Betz (ed.), *The Greek Magical Papyri in Translation, Including the Demotic Spells*, Second Edition (Chicago: University of Chicago Press, 1996), p. 130 (VII.429-458 at 451).

> The resolution is completed by the provision of a quasi-narrative link between the decoded elements, which converts the six 'words' into a theological hint. The *grammata* turn out really to be a cryptic form of natural theology; their power is of a wholly intelligible kind. They are the remnants of an ancient wisdom, the flotsam of a lost deep knowledge."[12]

Not all scholars agree on this, however, as we shall see in turn below. It would be my own contention that this knowledge has not been entirely lost, and that some aspects of it can be further reconstructed, or at least re-envisioned in a useful manner for modern polytheistic practitioners.

One interesting account of the Ephesia Grammata involves the Lydian king Kroisos (often spelled Croesus), whose name even in antiquity was connected proverbially to fabulous wealth—

---

[12] Gordon, p. 239.

indeed, it was Kroisos who innovated standardized coinage, and thus "invented" money as we know it, in the sixth century BCE. In the scholiast and lexicographers who cite this information about Kroisos in relation to the Ephesia Grammata, they all state that the letters themselves are charms that are difficult to understand, and that Kroisos spoke them when he was on the pyre.[13] This story needs to be explained a bit further in context.

The pyre spoken of in the accounts about Kroisos and the Ephesia Grammata was the pyre built by Cyrus, after the sacking of Sardis by his Persian army, upon which Kroisos was to die. Most modern scholars agree that this was probably the occasion of the king's death, but as Kroisos was

---

[13] Kotansky, p. 111, though the relevant excerpt from Plutarch in which this is said to have been recorded, as given on the "Healing and Protection" webpage (see note 1 above) does not state this information; a similar situation occurs with Rachel Lesser, "The Nature of Artemis Ephesia," *Hirundo: The McGill Journal of Classical Studies* 4 (2005-2006), pp. 43-54 at 47. McCown, p. 131, cites the *Suda*, Photius, and the scholiast Eustathius for this information, which can be found on the "Healing and Protection" webpage, as previously noted.

mythologized in various ways not long after his death, this situation for his demise would not do. Various accounts state that as he was on the pyre, he called out "Solon!" several times, and when Cyrus inquired what god this was, it was explained that Kroisos had an interview with Solon earlier in which he asked to know who was the happiest person alive, expecting Solon to state that it was Kroisos because of the happiness his wealth brought him, but Solon did not answer as expected. In his moment of painful death, therefore, Kroisos called out to him in remembrance of that painful lesson, and it is said that Cyrus was so impressed with this that he rescued Kroisos from the pyre and honored him, even making him an advisor at his court.[14]

The version of this story given in Herodotus says that Cyrus' men could not put out the flames on the pyre, and that instead Kroisos called out to Apollon and reminded him of the rich offerings he had given at Delphi, and a sudden rainstorm

---

[14] From Plutarch's *Life of Solon*: John Dryden (trans.), *Plutarch, The Lives of the Noble Grecians and Romans*, revised by Arthur Hugh Clough (New York: Modern Library, 1864), pp. 113-115.

extinguished the blaze, which impressed Cyrus.[15] A further version is given in Bacchylides' third ode, in which it is said that Apollon saved Kroisos from the pyre and delivered him and his daughters to safety and eternal reward in Hyperborea.[16] The connection between Apollon, Hyberborea, and Artemis is an interesting one: perhaps the uttering of the Ephesia Grammata was the method via which Kroisos was able to gain Apollon's attention for his intervention, whether as a rain-giver or as a deliverer to the beautiful lands beyond Thrace and the North Wind.

But, what is Kroisos' connection to Ephesus? In Herodotus, we are told (I.26): "The first Greeks [Kroisos] attacked were the Ephesians. It was during his siege that the Ephesians dedicated the city to Artemis by running a rope from the

---

[15] Robin Waterfield (trans.), *Herodotus, The Histories* (Oxford and New York: Oxford University Press, 1998), p. 40 (I.87).
[16] Sir Richard C. Jebb (ed./trans.), *Bacchylides, The Poems and Fragments* (Cambridge: Cambridge University Press, 1905), pp. 256-261.

outside wall to the temple."[17] However, based on Herodotus' later comments concerning the benefactions given to various cities by Kroisos,[18] it has been agreed that Kroisos did the first restoration of the ancient temple of Artemis at Ephesus in 550 BCE, making it one of the Seven Wonders of the Ancient World. We should understand that the textual traditions citing the Ephesia Grammata's provision of assistance to Kroisos (perhaps as a result of a misunderstanding of "Solon! Solon!" for *askion, kataskion*?) are late and obscure, and well passed the time when Kroisos' life and exploits had been heavily mythologized, so any conjectures on how he may have come into contact with the Ephesia Grammata in the mid-sixth century BCE, if indeed they were known at that time, is intriguingly suggestive at best.

It seems logical that it would have either been as a result of being impressed with the Ephesians' trust in their goddess and her sacred image, or as

---

[17] Waterfield, p. 12.
[18] Waterfield, p. 43 (I.92).

a result of his rebuilding the temple, that he came into contact with the Ephesia Grammata written on her statue. The pre-Hellenic cult statue of Ephesian Artemis, which Kallimachos says the locals called "Upis" and which may indeed be the original name of the goddess at that site,[19] was said to have been a wooden image, but it is also said to have fallen from heaven.[20] But, interestingly, the only ancient text in which this heavenly origin is stated explicitly is a Christian one, specifically *Acts of the Apostles* 19:35, "Citizens of Ephesus, who is there that does not know that the city of the Ephesians is the temple-keeper of the great Artemis and of the statue that fell from heaven?"[21] Her distinctive image—though it has been interpreted as many-breasted,

---

[19] Lesser, p. 46; Jan M. Bremmer, "Priestly Personnel of the Ephesian Artemision: Anatolian, Persian, Greek, and Roman Aspects" (2008), pp. 1-21 at 5, available at
http://theoi.eldoc.ub.rug.nl/FILES/root/2008/Priestly/Bremmer-Priests.pdf .

[20] Axel W. Persson, *The Religion of Greece in Prehistoric Times* (Berkeley and Los Angeles: The University of California Press, 1942), p. 143.

[21] The meaning of the final phrase in Greek, however, is uncertain, and being that it is the crucial one, this matter is therefore much less straightforward than it has often been presented.

strewn with bull's testicles, covered in eggs, or perhaps bee cocoons—may in fact indicate amber beads or bulb-like leather bags that were worn by a variety of deities in an Anatolian context, which Sarah B. Morris interprets as a "shaggy" Anatolian counterpart to the Greek golden fleece or the *aegis*.[22] While this is certainly possible, if the original cult image had indeed fallen from the heavens at some stage (and the revering of meteoric stones is certainly not unheard of in Anatolia and the Near East), perhaps the uneven shape of such meteoric stones suggested the image to those that may have later created a wooden version.

Returning to the matter of the Ephesia Grammata being the "Orphic formula," one is prompted to explore some further connections in this regard. Recalling that the Androkydes cited by Clement of Alexandria was said to have been a Pythagorean, and knowing the close connection

---

[22] Sarah P. Morris, "Potnia Aswiya: Anatolian Contributions to Greek Religion," in Robert Laffineur and Robin Hagg (eds.), *Potnia: Deities and Religion in the Aegean Bronze Age* (Liege: Universite de Liege, 2011), pp. 423-434 at 430-432.

of Pythagorean philosophy to Orphism, and the connection (if not derivation) of both of these from likely Thracian sources, it would be interesting to see if there is any other connection between the Ephesia Grammata and Orphic sources in particular. In Euripides' *Alcestis*, the chorus laments that there is nothing stronger than Ananke, the goddess of absolute necessity and destiny, including "the medicine contained in the Thracian tablets that the voice of Orpheus has inscribed."[23] Orpheus' repute as a magician and mystery tradition initiator is widespread, and the amulet-like gold lamellae as well as bone inscriptions that are characterized as "Orphic" in origin[24] form an extensive catalogue of myth,

---

[23] Fritz Graf and Sarah Iles Johnston, *Ritual Texts for the Afterlife: Orpheus and the Bacchic Gold Tablets* (London and New York: Routledge, 2007), p. 170; Christopher A. Faraone, "Mystery Cults and Incantations: Evidence for Orphic Charms in Euripides' Cyclops 646-48?" *Rheinisches Museum* 151 (2008) 127-142 at 131.

[24] See Graf and Johnston; Alberto Bernabé and Ana Isabel Jiménez San Cristóbal, *Instructions for the Netherworld: The Orphic Gold Tablets* (Leiden: E. J. Brill, 2008); Yannis Tzifopoulos, *'Paradise' Earned: The Bacchic-Orphic Gold Lamellae of Crete* (Cambridge: Harvard University Press, 2010); Alexis Pinchard, "The Salvific Function of Memory in Archaic Poetry, in the Orphic Gold Tablets, and in Plato: What Continuity, What Break?" The ISNS Tenth International Conference, Cagliari (2012), available at

mystery tradition, and magical *historiolae*. Amulets containing the Ephesia Grammata, which were current in the same locations and periods as the Orphic tablets, seem somewhat comparable to these, only they are always lead. A particular magical text from the *Greek Magical Papyri* corpus which features the Ephesia Grammata, to be detailed in the next chapter, has certain similarities to an Orphic-like initiatory text like those found on the lamellae.[25] Are the Ephesia Grammata among the other magical words, medicinal in their possible uses and implications, encompassed by the words of the chorus in Euripides' play? It seems possible, though far from certain.

Before closing this quick survey of the general features of the Ephesia Grammata's long historical traditions and associations, it would be useful to briefly assess the most recent academic hypotheses on the origins of the Ephesia

---

http://www.academia.edu/1621447/The_Salvific_Function_of_Memory_in_the_Archaic_Poetry_in_the_Orphic_Gold_Tablets_and_in_Plato_What_Continuity_What_Break .

[25] Faraone, "Mystery Cults," p. 132.

Grammata. Everything in this chapter before the present paragraph has been in an effort to understand how a person in late antiquity—say, the third or fourth century CE—might have understood the Ephesia Grammata amidst a vast web of associations to Ephesus and Artemis, to Orpheus, to Pythagoreanism, to Thrace, to the Daktyls (to be discussed further in a subsequent chapter), and a variety of other matters. But, the ways in which modern scholars view these matters is quite different, and in fact contradicts or disproves much of the above (though on certain matters, there is still some debate). As modern practitioners of polytheism, we live in a middle ground between the mythopoeic reality of our ancestors and the more prosaic but historically informed world of modernity and its standards of (amongst other things) valid academic evidence and argumentation. It behooves us to make an informed decision on which world we prefer to inhabit in a given circumstance, so in the interests of presenting as many options as possible to readers and users of this material, I offer the following summaries of the most recent discussions of the Ephesia

Grammata (many of which were not accessible to me until the very latest stages of writing the present volume).

David R. Jordan and Christopher A. Faraone speak for the general consensus when they state that an origin for the first two words of the traditional six Ephesia Grammata, *aski kataski*, can perhaps be discerned in a Greek hexametric incantation that was well-known in Sicily, Crete, and Magna Graecia in the late classical period (3rd or 4th century BCE), found on a lead tablet now in Cologne, but in severely corrupted form. The spell in question is very similar to a spell from the Great Magical Papyrus of Paris (a.k.a. *PGM* IV), a further example from Antinoöpolis, and several others.[26] The section of the incantation's verses begins, in Greek, εσκε κατα σκιερων; a

---

[26] Hans Dieter Betz (ed./trans.), *The Greek Magical Papyri in Translation, Including the Demotic Spells*, Second Edition (Chicago and London: The University of Chicago Press, 1996), IV.296-466, pp. 44-47. The spell from Antinoöpolis can be found in Mary Beard, John North, & Simon Price (eds./trans.), *Religions of Rome, Volume 2: A Sourcebook* (Cambridge: Cambridge University Press, 1998), pp. 266-267; Ogden, *Magic, Witchcraft, and Ghosts*, pp. 250-251; Gager, pp. 97-100.

translation of the relevant portion of the incantation reads:

> When under the shadowy mountains in the dark-gleaming land a child leads of necessity from the garden of Persephone at milking time the holy four-footed servant of Demeter, the goat with her ceaseless flow of rich milk...demanding torches for Hekate Einodia and with terrible voice the shouting goddess leads the stranger to the god...[27]

The connections of this passage as an *historiola* to Orphic imagery, mystery initiations, and a variety of other matters secures the context of the original two words from the Ephesia Grammata in an atmosphere of mystery religions and the magico-religious practices that can accompany them, which is the argument of Alberto

---

[27] David R. Jordan, "A Love Charm with Verses," *Zeitschrift für Papyrologie und Epigraphik* 72 (1988), pp. 245-259; Faraone, "Mystery Cults," pp. 132-133.

Bernabé.[28] The origins of the other four letters/words are explained by Bernabé as eventual distortions, often based on metrical and rhyme concerns, for phrases from an original dactylic hexametric verse, which included the further rhymed pair *aix tetrax* (with the first resulting from confusion between *ΑΙΞ* and *ΛΙΞ*), both ultimately deriving from "goat," *aasia endasia*, meaning "madness, disaster, folly" (later changed to *aisia*, "auspicious, favorable") and "hairy" respectively, and finally the insertion of *damnameneus* as a well-known entity that has metrically pleasing quasi-self-rhyming syllables, with a transparent etymology meaning "the one who subdues."[29] Further, the attribution of them to the geographical location of Ephesus is incorrect, and instead we should think of them as the *ephésia grámmata*, "liberating letters," due to

---

[28] Alberto Bernabé, "The *Ephesia Grammata*: Genesis of a Magical Formula," in Christopher A. Faraone and Dirk Obbink (eds.), *The Getty Hexameters: Poetry, Magic, and Mystery in Ancient Selinous* (Oxford and New York: Oxford University Press, 2013), pp. 71-95 at 90-93.

[29] Bernabé, pp. 85-90, 93-95.

their effectiveness in protective spells, healing magic, and the like.[30]

Radcliffe G. Edmonds III, however, disagrees on the Orphic nature of the Ephesia Grammata, since the one definite connection to the Orphic sphere in the *PGM* spell calling it the "Orphic formula" is late (fourth century CE). Citing the verses which contain the Ephesia Grammata in the Getty Hexameters text that dates from the fourth century BCE, which attribute the formula directly to Paean Apollon, Edmonds instead connects the formula to Apollon in his healing and harm-averting role, and likewise to Hekate (as in another of the *PGM* spells to be discussed subsequently).[31] This strengthens the attestation of the Ephesia Grammata's usage by Kroisos and the abundant connections to Apollon in the

---

[30] Bernabé, p. 94.
[31] Radcliffe G. Edmonds III, "The *Ephesia Grammata: Logos Orphaïkos* or APolline *Alexima Pharmaka*?" in Christopher A. Faraone and Dirk Obbink (eds.), *The Getty Hexameters: Poetry, Magic, and Mystery in Ancient Selinous* (Oxford and New York: Oxford University Press, 2013), pp. 97-106.

various stories of his fate upon Cyrus' pyre, even though these are most likely ahistorical.

Another theory, proposed by Sarah P. Morris, is that the Ephesia Grammata derive from Hittite sources in the original Anatolian geographic context of Ephesus itself.[32] The carrying of the Ephesia Grammata in leather bags, which will be discussed in a subsequent chapter, might connect to the animal skin pouches possibly depicted on Artemis of Ephesus' cult image, as suggested by Morris. This could be the case, certainly, though it is somewhat more difficult to prove, and is not the position of the scholars mentioned above.

With any luck, this initial chapter has served—to paraphrase Androkydes' words as quoted by Clement of Alexandria—to lead one from the "shadowless" darkness around the Ephesia Grammata into realms less dark but still "shadowy." The chapter to follow this one will

---

[32] Morris, pp. 432-433. Morris suggests on p. 433, note 64, that she will pursue the Hittite origins of the Ephesia Grammata further in a future article, but I am not currently aware of that article having been published as of the completion of the present volume.

continue in this fashion, moving into the more solid "earth" and the times and turning "seasons" in which the Ephesia Grammata are found in spell texts and inscriptions. Next, we shall proceed to the undefeated light of the "sun" in terms of the Ephesia Grammata's usage as protective amulets, whether materially inscribed or spoken. After that, we will examine the "true voice/word" and the voices behind the Ephesia Grammata as actual divine beings of some sort. Finally, we will move into the territory not described by Androkydes, as we "kindle hairy distributors" (!?!) in terms of exploring the usage of the Ephesia Grammata as a system of divination.

LIX, TETRAX:

"Earth, Seasons"

Examples of the Ephesia Grammata in Ancient Texts

WHAT follows in the present chapter is a survey and catalogue—though far from a complete one[33]—of the appearances of the Ephesia Grammata in various magical texts of the ancient world. The present instance will not include the prose mentions of the Ephesia Grammata detailed in the previous chapter, but instead will focus on texts in which the Ephesia Grammata are used as parts of spells for various purposes in a direct fashion.

---

[33] Several more such examples are unavailable to me at present, including some detailed in the new book on the Getty Hexameters, and catalogued in Alberto Bernabé, "The *Ephesia Grammata*: Genesis of a Magical Formula," in Christopher A. Faraone and Dirk Obbink (eds.), *The Getty Hexameters: Poetry, Magic, and Mystery in Ancient Selinous* (Oxford and New York: Oxford University Press, 2013), pp. 71-95, as only a portion of that chapter has been accessible to me as of the publication of the present volume.

One of the oldest appearances of the Ephesia Grammata is at the beginning of a lead tablet containing a *defixio* from Himera, dating to the fifth century BCE.[34] A further text from Lokroi is similar, dating to the fourth century BCE, but rather than being a *defixio*, it is more of an *epoidai* or "spell" which has mystical implications.[35] These, in turn, are also similar to a further lead tablet found in Phalasarna in Crete and also dating to the fourth century BCE.[36] It reads as follows:

> Messenger…up…I bid you to flee from these houses of ours….I call on Zeus Averter of evil and on Herakles Sacker of cities and on the Healer and on Victory and on Apollo. Ah, ah, thus Tetragos (the goat) drags the PUXUTUAITAGALIS. Epaphos, Epaphos, Epaphos, flee; She-wolf, flee also; And you, Dog, and PROKROPROSATE (the Thief?),…

---

[34] David R. Jordan, "Ephesia Grammata at Himera," *Zeitschrift für Papyrologie und Epigraphik* 130 (2000), pp. 104–107.

[35] David R. Jordan, "Three Texts from Lokroi Epizephyrioi," *Zeitschrift für Papyrologie und Epigraphik* 130 (2000), pp. 95–103.

[36] David R. Jordan, "The Inscribed Lead Tablet from Phalasarna," *Zeitschrift für Papyrologie und Epigraphik* 94 (1992), pp. 191–194.

associate. Let them run maddened, each to his own house. Oath...dog. Aski Kataski {Kataski} AASIAN ENDASIAN "at milking time," goat... "drive from the garden by force the goat." To whom the name is Tetragos, and to you the name Trex...windy promontory. Happy is he for whom has been scattered, along the highway IO! PHRESILLUTO (Shorn of his senses?) let him have the cry of the blessed along the highway. Trax Tetrax Tetragos. Damnameneu...tame by force the wickedly unwilling, whoever hurts me and those who KOLLOBALOUSI (cast as a binding spell??) evil things—hawk-wing, PELEIOPETON (dove feather?), entirely mixed AMISANTON of the Chimera, claw of lion, tongue of bearded lion-serpent—shall not harm me with ointment or application or with drink or with spell, spoiler of all things.[37]

---

[37] This translation is given, based on Jordan's text, at the "Healing and Protection" webpage noted in footnote 1 above.

That Zeus, Herakles, Nike/Victoria, and Paean Apollon are all called upon in this spell is intriguing; but, the reference toward the end to the "bearded lion-serpent" might suggest the Judeo-Graeco-Egyptian syncretistic deity Chnoubis.[38] The so-called Getty Hexameters, dating from the fifth century BCE and likely from Selinous in Sicily, reads as follows:

> ...and I do not utter the profane. Who hides in a house of stone the visible letters of these holy words, inscribed on a tin sheet, what the broad earth feeds or loud-roaring Amphitrite nurtures in the sea shall not harm him.
>
> *Paean, you send medicines that ward off everything,*
> *indeed speaking these immortal words to mortals:*

---

[38] Howard M. Jackson, *The Lion Becomes Man: The Gnostic Leontomorphic Creator and the Platonic Tradition* (Atlanta: Scholar's Press, 1985); Atilio Mastrocinque, *From Jewish Magic to Gnosticism*, Studien und Texte zu Antike und Christentum 24 (Tübingen: Mohr Siebeck, 2005).

...down from shadowy mountains in a dark-gleaming land a child brings from Persephone's garden for milking, by necessity, the four-footed holy servant of Demeter, a nanny laden with an unceasing flow of rich milk, and she (the nanny) follows, trusting in the bright goddesses ... torches, and Hecate Enodia, shouting a foreign-sounding shout in a terrifying voice, does, herself a goddess, point out to a god the way.

... 'I come self-bidden through the ... night, and coming forth from the chambers I say to gods immortal and to mortals the god-spoken things of the bright-fruited deity ....'

...announcing to them to keep their hands from impious burnt offerings.'

Paean, for you yourself send warding-off medicines.

'And hear in their hearts the sweet [——] of

the voice: I order you to make incantation over mortal men, both in war and not in war and on ships, whenever death-bringing Bane comes upon all men and upon flocks and mortal issue, indeed thus to make incantation night and day ....'

Paean, you ward off and are good.

'Aski Kataski Kataski Aassia Asia Endasian ... – towards milking – Aix. Borne on the wind, drive out the she-goat from the garden by force. {Your name is Tetragos ....} Blessed is he on whom this (shout) "Iô" was scattered along the highway, and who keeps in his heart the voice of the blessed along the highway, "Trax Tetrax Tetragos". Damnameneus, subdue by necessity, though, those foully unwilling.'

'[I come self-bidd]en through the ... night ....' '[Heracle]s son of Zeus [——] all-unlucky day. [Knowing] is he who remembers Zeus and far-shooting Ph[oebus] and [Heracles'] bows and indeed the many-headed Hydra:'

Paean, for he himself sends warding-off medicines.

'No harm would she do, not even should she come with much medicine.'[39]

In this, we not only see the hexameter verses referring to the shadow of the dark mountain upon which the Ephesia Grammata are thought to have been based by modern scholars, but also most of the canonical Ephesia Grammata themselves incorporated later into the text of the incantation. Paean Apollon plays a large role as the source of the incantation itself, but likewise Zeus, Herakles, Phoebus Apollon, Persephone, Demeter, and Hekate Enodia also play a role in the text. To review briefly, the original hexameters are thought to have dated from the fifth century BCE, and an example of them was found in the midst of a third- or fourth-century

---

[39] David R. Jordan and Roy Kotansky, "Ritual Hexameters in the Getty Museum: Preliminary Edition," *Zeitschrift für Papyrologie und Epigraphik* 178 (2011), pp. 54-62 at 57-61.

BCE love spell from Oxyrhynchus in Egypt, the relevant section of which runs as follows:

> ...Nature-roamer, night-roamer, I order you, "Dog, Serpent, Chaplet, Key, Caduceus, bronze sandal of the ruler of Tartarus, gold sandal of De[...]prus; having seen the iron-sandalled female I fled and went in the tracks of the gold-sandalled Kore; save me, savior of the cosmos, daughter of Demeter," to activate this charm for me: drive, spell-bind Matrona, whom Tagene bore, whose substance you have, whom Theodorus, whom Techosis bore, has in mind— "When under the shadowy mountains in the dark-gleaming land the child drives by force from the garden of Persephone at milking time the holy four-footed servant of Demeter, the goat with her ceaseless flow of rich milk THESOMENON... torches for Hecate Einodia; with a terrible voice the barbarously shouting goddess leads to the god; Night, Erebos, Darkness, Aion, Light, Artemis chaste ... four-footed

> ... Aphrodite delighting in her girdle, Persephoneia, Phoebe, ... arrow-pourer ... provident, arrow-tamer."—keep this spell unbreakable forever.[40]

Again, we see Hekate Enodia here associated with the formula, as well as Persephone and Demeter, Artemis, Aphrodite, Nyx, Erebos, Aion, and others.

Several spells from the corpus of the *Greek Magical Papyri* (*PGM*) also use the Ephesia Grammata, or at least parts of it. From *PGM* VII, dating to the third or fourth century CE, we find the following:

> **A restraining rite for anything**, works even on chariots. It also causes enmity and sickness, cuts down, destroys, and overturns, for whatever you wish. The spell in it, when said, conjures daimons out and makes them enter objects or people.

---

[40] David R. Jordan, "A Love Charm with Verses," *Zeitschrift für Papyrologie und Epigraphik* 72 (1988), pp. 245-259 at 252-253.

Engrave in a plate made of lead from a cold-water channel what you want to happen, and when you have consecrated it with bitter aromatics such as myrrh, bdellium, styrax, and aloes and thyme, with river mud, late in the evening or in the middle of the night, where there is a stream or the drain of a bath, having tied a cord to the plate throw it into the stream—or into the sea—and let it be carried along. Use the cord so that, when you wish, you can undo the spell. Then should you wish to break the spell, untie the plate. Say the formula seven times and you will see something wonderful. Then go away without turning back or giving an answer to anyone, and when you have washed and immersed yourself, go up to your own room and rest, and use only vegetable food. Write the spell with a headless bronze needle.

The text to be written is: "I conjure you, lord Osiris, by your holy names OUCHIOCH OUSENARATH, Osiris,

OUSERRANNOUPHTHI OSORNOUPHE Osiris Mnevis, OUSERSETEMENTH AMARA MACHI CHOMASO EMMAI SERBONI EMER Isis, ARATOPHI ERACHAX ESEOIOTH ARBIOTHI AMEN CHNOUM MONMONT OUZATHI PER OUNNEPHER EN OOO, I give over to you, lord Osiris, and I deposit with you this matter" (add the usual).

But if you cause the plate to be buried or sunk in river or land or sea or stream or coffin or in a well, write the Orphic formula, saying "ASKEI KAI TASKEI" and, taking a black thread, made 365 knots and bind the thread around the outside of the plate, saying the same formula again and, "Keep him who is held," or whatever you do. And thus the plate is deposited. For Selene, when she goes through the underworld, breaks whatever spell she finds. But when this rite has been performed, the spell remains unbroken so long as you say over the formula daily at the spot where the plate is deposited. Do

> not hastily share this information with anyone, for you will find its like only with much labor.[41]

Given that this is our only source that directly connects the Ephesia Grammata with the Orphic tradition, it is interesting to see that it takes place in the context of a spell to the Egyptian deities Osiris (and, to a much lesser extent, Isis), and which only mentions Selene in passing for explanatory purposes.

A further *PGM* spell (LXX), also from the third or fourth century CE, has been discussed by a variety of scholars as a possible remnant of a *katabasis* ritual, involving travel to the underworld for initiatory purposes,[42] and which

---

[41] Hans Dieter Betz (ed.), *The Greek Magical Papyri in Translation, Including the Demotic Spells*, Second Edition (Chicago: University of Chicago Press, 1996), pp. 129-130 (VII.429-458).

[42] Roy Kotansky, "Incantations and Prayers for Salvation on Inscribed Greek Amulets," in Christopher A. Faraone and Dirk Obbink (eds.), *Magika Hiera: Ancient Greek Magic & Religion* (Oxford and New York: Oxford University Press, 1991), pp. 107-137 at 121; Christopher A. Faraone, "Mystery Cults and Incantations: Evidence for Orphic Charms in Euripides' Cyclops 646-48?" *Rheinisches Museum* 151 (2008) 127-142 at 132; Hans Dieter Betz, "Fragments

features Hekate in a syncretized form as Hekate Ereshkigal.[43]

> **Charm of Hekate Ereschigal against fear of punishment.** If he comes forth, say to him: "I am Ereschigal, the one holding her thumbs, and not even one evil can befall her."
>
> If, however, he comes close to you, take hold of your right heel and recite the following: "Ereschigal, virgin, bitch, serpent, wreath, key, cadeucus, golden sandal of the ruler of Tartaros." And you will avert him.
>
> "ASKEI KATASKEI ERON OREON

---

from a Catabasis Ritual in a Greek Magical Papyrus," *History of Religions* 19.4 (May 1980), pp. 287-295; Jake Stratton-Kent, *Geosophia: The Argo of Magic*, 2 Volumes (Dover: Scarlet Imprint, 2010), Vol. 2, pp. 56-58.

[43] For more on the Graeco-Egyptian syncretisms of Ereshkigal, see P. Sufenas Virius Lupus, "Ereshkigal in the Graeco-Roman-Egyptian Magical Tradition," in Tess Dawson (ed.), *Anointed: A Devotional Anthology for the Deities of the Near and Middle East* (Bibliotheca Alexandrina, 2011), pp. 213-224.

IOR MEGA SAMNYER BAUI (3 times) PHOBANTIA SEMNE. I have been initiated, and I went down into the chamber of the Dactyls, and I saw the other things down below, virgin, bitch, and all the rest." Say it at the crossroad, and turn around and flee, because it is at those places that she appears. Saying it late at night, about what you wish, it will reveal it in your sleep; and if you are led away to death, say it while scattering seeds of sesame, and it will save you.

"PHORBA PHORBA BRIMO AZZIEBYA." Take bran of first quality and sandalwood and vinegar of the sharpest sort and mold a cake. And write the name of so-and-so upon it, and insvribe it in such a way that you speak over it into the light the name of Hekate, and this: "Take away his sleep from such-and-such a person," and he will be

39

sleepless and worried.[44]

The two initial Ephesia Grammata used in the formula here follow the pattern of the hexametric verses mentioned earlier, and in fact the whole of the *voces magicae* at that part could translate to "When beneath the shadowy mountains IOR great SAMNYER barking" followed by "terrifying, august/awe-inspiring one." Interestingly, one could argue that because the original context of that section of the spell may involve an underworld initiation, this would link the spell to Orphic tradition as well, and the things which Orpheus may have seen on such a *katabasis*.

The connections of Hekate to the Ephesia Grammata brings us to a final conjectural example, which may be the chronologically earliest.[45] A fragmentary fifth-century BCE monument contains a circular inscribed stone like

---

[44] Betz, *Greek Magical Papyri*, pp. 297-298 (LXX.4-25).
[45] John G. Gager, *Curse Tablets and Binding Spells from the Ancient World* (Oxford and New York: Oxford University Press, 1992), p. 6.

the base of a column, inscribed with a scroll and a ram, with much of the inscription illegible, and the following more clearly:

> The Ephesian vengeance was sent down. Firstly Hecate harms the belongings of Megara in all things, and then Persephone reports to the gods. All these things are already so.[46]

Lillian. H. Jeffery writes of this object, "Perhaps in this case the suppliant, whose *defixio* had been entirely successful, offered the stone in gratitude; on it he had a representation made of the leaden scroll bearing the original curse, and below came the details of the fulfillment."[47] While some letters are discernible in the possible *defixio* section, including the names of Ploutos and

---

[46] Daniel Ogden, "Binding Spells: Curse Tablets and Voodoo Dolls in the Greek and Roman Worlds," in Valerie Flint, Richard Gordon, Georg Luck, and Daniel Ogden, *Witchcraft and Magic in Europe, Volume 2: Ancient Greece and Rome* (London: The Athlone Press, 1999), pp. 1-90 at 47.

[47] Lillian H. Jeffery, "Further Comments on Archaic Greek Inscriptions," *The Annual of the British School at Athens* 50 (1955), pp. 67-84 at 75.

Persephone, it is not at all clear that what can be discerned otherwise, nor what may have remained which is now destroyed or illegible, is the canonical Ephesia Grammata in any recognizable form, despite Jeffery,[48] Gager, and Ogden's opinions on the matter (unless they were speaking more in terms of "Ephesia Grammata" being any variety of *voces magicae*).[49] However, the presence of the ram's head and the goat imagery found in the examples above, the mentioning of Hekate and Persephone, and the specific collocation "Ephesian vengeance" is highly suggestive.

Interestingly, Hekate is connected to Ephesus in another way, according to one ancient story. It is known as the tale of the "Wife of Ephesus," and it occurs in one source, a fragment attributed to Kallimachos from his *Hypomnemata*. The story details how a king called Ephesus (a ruler of that city) had in his house a woman who offended the

---

[48] Jeffery, pp. 75-76.
[49] Jeffery, p. 72, gives the mostly legible portion as Figure 2; the original is in Maximilian Fraenkel (ed.), *Inscriptiones Graecae* IV (Berlin: George Reimer, 1892), p. 73 §496.

goddess Artemis by refusing her hospitality and expelling her from the house. In anger, Artemis changed the woman into a bitch, but then felt pity for her and returned her to human form. The woman was ashamed and hung herself with her girdle, but Artemis removed her own finery and adorned the woman's corpse, naming her Hekate.[50] This compares to a tale in which the tyrant Pythagoras of Ephesus killed the Basilids, but allowed one girl to be spared, though she was confined to a temple; she hung herself to escape starvation, after which plague and famine struck the city, and the Delphic Oracle suggested erecting a temple and burying the dead. Joseph Fontenrose suggests that perhaps we are to understand that Artemis was in the form of the girl in this case.[51] This story fits several of the details, including the location, of the "Wife of Ephesus" tale. However, the Pythagoras of Ephesus story also compares quite closely to the

---

[50] Rudolf Pfeiffer, *Callimachus, Volumen 1: Fragmenta* (Oxford: Oxford University Press, 1949), pp. 352 §461.
[51] Joseph Fontenrose, *The Delphic Oracle, Its Responses and Operations, with a Catalogue of Responses* (Berkeley: University of California Press, 1978), pp. 76-77.

change of name for Iphigenia, a maiden who in the pre-Trojan War period was sacrificed to Artemis. The latter story, in terms of the specifics of the name change and the goddess who brings it about, also must be considered in juxtaposition with the "Wife of Ephesus" tale.[52] Are we to assume that the wife of Ephesus became the goddess, or merely an attendant for Artemis with the goddess Hekate's name? It is difficult to say whether or not there is more significance to this story from Kallimachos than what our single fragment indicates, but it is another intriguing occurrence of Hekate in relation to canid imagery and cynanthropy in particular.[53]

Hekate looms large in Greek tradition, appearing

---

[52] Jennifer Larson, *Greek Heroine Cults* (Madison: University of Wisconsin Press, 1995), pp. 153-154; Sarah Iles Johnston, *The Restless Dead: Encounters Between the Living and the Dead in Ancient Greece* (Berkeley: University of California Press, 1999), pp. 242-246.

[53] For further information on this topic, see Phillip A. Bernhardt-House, "Hekate's Bitch: Hecuba and Other Greek Traditions of Cynanthropy," in Sannion (ed.), *Bearing Torches: A Devotional Anthology for Hekate* (Eugene: Bibliotheca Alexandrina, 2009), pp. 46-55.

in the *Homeric Hymn to Demeter*[54] as well as Hesiod's *Theogony*,[55] and having pride of place in the *Orphic Hymns* at the very beginning of the collection.[56] She was also very important in the *Chaldean Oracles*.[57] She makes a striking epiphany in close association with hounds in Theocritus,[58] Apollonius of Rhodes' *Argonautika*,[59] Lukian of Samosata's *Philopseudes*,[60] and Nonnos of

---

[54] Apostolos N. Athanassakis (trans.), *The Homeric Hymns* (Baltimore and London: The Johns Hopkins University Press, 2004), pp. 2-3, 13-14.

[55] Glenn W. Most (trans.), *Hesiod, Theogony, Works and Days, Testimonia* (Cambridge: Harvard University Press, 2006), pp. 36-39.

[56] Apostolos N. Athanassakis and Benjamin M. Wolkow (trans.), *The Orphic Hymns* (Baltimore and London: The Johns Hopkins University Press, 2013), pp. 5, 73-75.

[57] Sarah Iles Johnston, *Hekate Soteira: A Study of Hekate's Roles in the Chaldean Oracles and Related Literature* (Atlanta: Scholars Press, 1990).

[58] George Luck (ed./trans.), *Arcana Mundi: Magic and the Occult in the Greek and Roman Worlds* (Baltimore and London: The Johns Hopkins University Press, 1985), p. 68; Saara Lilja, *Dogs in Ancient Greek Poetry* (Helsinki: Societas Scientiarum Fennica, 1976), p. 92.

[59] E. V. Rieu (trans.), *Apollonius of Rhodes, The Voyage of Argo* (London and New York: Penguin, 1971), pp. 136, 141; Lilja, p. 101.

[60] Daniel Ogden, *In Search of the Sorcerer's Apprentice: The Traditional Tales of Lucian's Lover of Lies* (Swansea: The Classical Press of Wales, 2007), pp. 50-51 (§13-15), 54-55 (§22-24).

Panopolis' *Dionysiaka*,[61] and her cultic appearances elsewhere are numerous.[62] She is also important in the practices of the modern Ekklesía Antínoou, and receives regular honors therein at all major rituals.[63] That she would be important in the overall assessment of the Ephesia Grammata, especially in its usage with the spell texts discussed in this chapter (and elsewhere in the *PGM* corpus),[64] and in connection with underworld journeys, initiations, and with the ever-present black chthonic canid imagery, seems obvious and worth keeping in mind in one's future work with the letters.

---

[61] W. H. D. Rouse (trans.), *Nonnos, Dionysiaca, Books I-XV* (Cambridge: Harvard University Press, 1984), pp. 104-107.

[62] Robert Von Rudloff, *Hekate in Ancient Greek Religion* (Victoria, B.C.: Horned Owl Publishing, 1999).

[63] P. Sufenas Virius Lupus, "Gatekeepers, Way-Clearers, Mediators: Wepwawet (or Anubis and Hermanubis), Hekate and Ianus in the Practices of the Ekklesía Antínoou," in Sannion (ed.), *Bearing Torches: A Devotional Anthology for Hekate* (Bibliotheca Alexandrina, 2009), pp. 169-178; *Devotio Antinoo: The Doctor's Notes, Volume 1* (Anacortes: The Red Lotus Library, 2011), pp. 112-113.

[64] Betz, *Greek Magical Papyri*, pp. 65 (the goddess is addressed as "O Black Bitch"), 75 (cow and dog heads), 92 (goat and dog heads); further, Brimo (often taken as a by-name of Hekate) is described as a "dog in maiden shape," as well as "wolf-formed" and "dog-shaped," in a spell on pp. 78-79.

From the darkness of the underworld and the changeability of the moon (associated with Hekate) and with magical operations to impact others related to the Ephesia Grammata, we now move to the usage of the letters for protective purposes, in the light of "the sun."

DAMNAMENEUS:
"Sun"

The Ephesia Grammata as Protective Amulets

IN addition to the *voces magicae* attestations of the Ephesia Grammata given in the previous chapter, the most frequent usage for the Ephesia Grammata in the ancient world was in a protective capacity, whether recited or inscribed on amulets of various sorts. This is certainly the context in which Kroisos was said to have used them, and which Radcliffe G. Edmonds III has suggested is the true origins of the formula, as witnessed in the first chapter of this book. Some of the lead spell tablets discussed in the previous chapter seem to have been carried as protective amulets.[65] A fragment from Menander suggests

---

[65] John G. Gager, *Curse Tablets and Binding Spells from the Ancient World* (Oxford and New York: Oxford University Press, 1992), p. 6.

that married couples used to employ the Ephesia Grammata to ward off evil during their nuptials.[66] Further, Plutarch suggests in his two passages mentioning the Ephesia Grammata that repeating them can afford protection and put fear to flight,[67] which McCown suggests is also found in a passage from Marcus Aurelius: "In the writings of the Ephesians was laid down the advice to have constantly in remembrance some one of the ancients who lived virtuously."[68]

---

[66] Chester C. McCown, "The Ephesia Grammata in Popular Belief," *Transactions and Proceedings of the American Philological Association* 54 (1923), pp. 128-140 at 128, 131; Daniel Ogden, "Binding Spells: Curse Tablets and Voodoo Dolls in the Greek and Roman Worlds," in Valerie Flint, Richard Gordon, Georg Luck, and Daniel Ogden, *Witchcraft and Magic in Europe, Volume 2: Ancient Greece and Rome* (London: The Athlone Press, 1999), pp. 1-90 at 47; Roy Kotansky, "Incantations and Prayers for Salvation on Inscribed Greek Amulets," in Christopher A. Faraone and Dirk Obbink (eds.), *Magika Hiera: Ancient Greek Magic & Religion* (Oxford and New York: Oxford University Press, 1991), pp. 107-137 at 111.. See also note 1, above, for the translated text of Menander's fragment.
[67] See also note 1, above, for the translated text of Plutarch.
[68] McCown, pp. 134-135 and note 26; C. R. Haines, *Marcus Aurelius* (Cambridge: Harvard University Press, 1930), pp. 316-317 (XI.26). This suggestion, it seems, has not been echoed by most later commentators.

Apart from speaking the Ephesia Grammata when needed (or simply doing so frequently as a matter of course), their written form was used for amuletic purposes. The inscribed form of the six letters could be carried in a variety of ways. Edward Falkener suggests that they were carried in a leather pouch on one's person, according to his interpretation of the lines from Anaxilas in Athenaeus' *Deipnosophistai*.[69] In Charles Burton Gulick's translation of the passage, however, we are told that the letters themselves were carried on bits of stitched leather,[70] while Roy Kotansky's translation suggests that they were carried "in little stitched hides."[71] Other sources indicate that the Ephesia Grammata were inscribed on knucklebones, which in one famous

---

[69] Edward Falkener, *Ephesus, and the Temple of Diana* (London: Day & Son, 1862), pp. 144-145. He references a "Metrical Proverbs" source for this same information, but I have not been able to locate it.
[70] Charles Burton Gulick (trans.), *Athenaeus, Volume V* (Cambridge: Harvard University Press, 1933), p. 486-487; Richard Gordon, "Imagining Greek and Roman Magic," in Valerie Flint, Richard Gordon, Georg Luck, and Daniel Ogden, *Witchcraft and Magic in Europe, Volume 2: Ancient Greece and Rome* (London: The Athlone Press, 1999), pp. 159-275 at 214.
[71] Kotansky, p. 111.

case mentioned in several ancient sources (the *Suda*, Eustathius, and Photius), allowed an Ephesian wrestler to be victorious over a Milesian, until the knucklebone was taken from him, whereupon he was beaten repeatedly.

For personal protection in the modern period, the Ephesia Grammata could even be tattooed on one's skin, perhaps. In its most appealing description, according to Randy Conner, the usual method of using the Ephesia Grammata for protective amulets was to inscribe them on wood in gold letters and carry them in a leather pouch.[72] While he bases this suggestion on the previously mentioned passage from Edward Falkener, there is nothing to suggest in that passage that this was the traditional method, and

---

[72] Randy P. Conner, *Blossom of Bone: Reclaiming the Connections Between Homoeroticism and the Sacred* (New York: HarperCollins Publishers, 1993), p. 96; essentially the same information is given in Randy P. Conner, David Hatfield Sparks and Mariya Sparks, *Cassell's Encyclopedia of Queer Myth, Symbol and Spirit: Covering Gay, Lesbian, Bisexual and Transgender Lore* (London and New York: Cassell, 1997), p. 230 s.v. Megabyzos. Conner gets the detail of gold being used for the letters via misreading "good" as "gold" in the Anaxilas passage from Athenaeus.

no source from the ancient world I have been able to locate at present suggests this. Nonetheless, it is an aesthetically pleasing suggestion to potentially adopt.

As gold is a bit harder to come by these days in certain respects, a potential alternative for modern usage would be to paint the letters in gold paint on wood, or use a gold glitter pen or other such writing device to create a similar effect. My first personal set of Ephesia Grammata was not in gold letters, but it has seemed to work for this purpose equally well as if I had been able to make them in gold. As with so many things, use your own discretion, and work with what tools you have easily to hand—it is far better to start using the system in an imperfect or non-ideal form than to put it off indefinitely until one has the perfect pieces of wood, the nicest gold paint, the time to melt gold foil into carved or wood-burned grooves, and so forth.

The most regular usage I have for the Ephesia Grammata, which I do on a daily basis, involves both the pronunciation of the words several times a day, carrying them inscribed on wood in a leather pouch, and doing a particular short ritual with them involving gestures as well as their chanting. This ritual was something I spontaneously did in a dream early in the morning on January 8th, 2013. As January 8th is (amongst other things) a festival in the Ekklesía Antínoou dedicated to Pan's syncretism with Antinous,[73] and the *panic* associated with Pan is something that comes up from time to time, it is not a surprise that this dream was a fearful one, and necessitated an action for protection. I give below the account I wrote later on that day from my dream journal.

> Oftentimes, the first dream of the night that I have is a kind of bad dream—it's usually during the first 30 minutes to hour of sleep I have, I wake up in a start, and then am awake for a short while and get back to sleep. I can't quite remember what the dream was initially, but

---

[73] P. Sufenas Virius Lupus, *Devotio Antinoo: The Doctor's Notes, Volume 1* (Anacortes: The Red Lotus Library, 2011), pp. 119-120.

somehow, demons (as in "bad spiritual beings," not *daimones* in general) were involved. Within the dream, I woke up to a whole crowd of demons right in front of my face/hovering above me. I jumped out of bed, and looked out my window (which wasn't my window…or, at least, wasn't *quite* my window now), and I could see the moon on the horizon—and, consistently, in my dreams, the moon is larger than it usually is in person by several orders of magnitude…and, it was also in the wrong place, because it would never be close to the horizon to the SE, but anyway, I wasn't thinking of that. I felt I needed to do something to get rid of the demons, so I basically did this weird quasi-Shinto version of the LBRP (which I've never done in my life), but it used the Ephesia Grammata as well…?!? And, as I did it each time, the moon kept changing, first from a gibbous moon, and then it became a crescent, and then finally it sort of broke open and shone despite being a dark moon…it was like it opened a hole in the universe or something. I was then yelling and running around the house rejoicing that "I did it! I did it!" and woke up Rufus [one of my dogs]. And then I woke up for real, and felt really uneasy, and had to clear the "dream-lines" out of my waking vision for a few minutes before I could settle down and get back to sleep.

So, the next question is: do I start practicing that Shinto-LBRP-Ephesia Grammata ritual on a regular basis, or just assume it's dream drivel and forget about it?…

I suspect, given that I'm going to be doing an Antinoan Dream Incubation ritual at PantheaCon, I'm being put through my paces a bit this month…

My musings on the latter subjects were correct: not only did this short ritual practice become a part of the Antinoan Dream Incubation ritual at

PantheaCon 2013 (on which, more later), but it also became a regular part of my practices. This became especially so after the early part of April 2013, when I was told in an oracular session with the Norse god Freyr that this practice should become something I do every day. Between early January and early April of 2013, I mainly used the ritual when I was going to be away from my home shrine for overnight trips, in order to protect it from physical harm as well as any negative energies of the other people who live at or near my place of residence.

On the trip back from PantheaCon 2013, I ended up using it while I was in the security line at the airport. I had forgotten that a small pocketknife that was my grandfather's, which I carry as a reminder of my ancestors, was still in my pocket and not in my checked baggage. Fearing that it might be confiscated, I unobtrusively performed the ritual on the carry-on bag where I had placed it, hoping to make it invisible to the security personnel. That bag was not searched by security; however, my other carry-on bag was randomly searched because they did not know what to make of a small Ark of the Covenant replica that carried small statues of Antinous and Wepwawet and other important sacred objects(!?!), and because there was a can of diet soda in one of the pockets of that bag which I swore I had taken out earlier so as not to get trouble from security. Whether the knife was actively invisible to them, or the distraction with the other bag was created to focus their attention elsewhere, I am not sure—the point is, it worked!

When I first did a workshop on the Ephesia Grammata at PantheaCon 2014, I also found myself using my ritual and simply chanting the words repeatedly throughout the convention for protective purposes. I also used the ritual above in a spontaneous healing spell/prayer for Margot Adler during a larger communal ritual with individual contributions for the purpose of her healing (which she found very intriguing!), and likewise as part of the procedure in the Beard Blessing Ritual that I performed on the final day of the conference. At least one potentially difficult situation that might have happened involving me at PantheaCon in 2014 was averted entirely. Once the convention was over, I saw Margot Adler, with whom I had been interacting a few hours earlier (and had likewise done so on several other occasions over the weekend), and yet she did not initially recognize me. I wonder if this, too, was part of the effects of the Ephesia Grammata's usage: that it made me effectively "invisible" even when I was right in front of someone on certain occasions during this period. Who is to know for certain?

The "Shinto LBRP" ritual is noted as such by me in the above dream journal entry because of two things about the practice as it first emerged: the use of similar actions or gestures in a triadic pattern to encompass past, present, and future is a feature of a variety of Shinto practices, from the *temizu* to the use of the *haraegushi* wand (both of which are for purification);[74] and the use of the Lesser Banishing Ritual of the Pentagram in

---

[74] Ann Llewellyn Evans, *Shinto Norito: A Book of Prayers* (Victoria: Matsuri Foundation of Canada, 2001), pp. 116-119.

ceremonial magic.[75] In the version of this that I used in the dream, three different stars are done in succession: first, an upright pentagram with the six Ephesia Grammata said at each point (thus when the first point is returned to in tracing the figure, the sixth word is said at the same place as the first); then an inverted pentagram with the six Ephesia Grammata said at each point; and finally a di-triangular (non-unicursal) hexagram in which each point is emphasized with the speaking of the Ephesia Grammata. There is more to my own practice of this, including different mudra-like hand gestures representing aspects of Antinous,[76] use of different hands, starting at particular points of the various stars, breathing in a particular fashion, and "reaching through" the centers of the different stars that are drawn at the close of each

---

[75] Johan August Alm, *Tartaros: On the Orphic and Pythagorean Underworld, and the Pythagorean Pentagram* (Hercules, CA: Three Hands Press, 2013), pp. 111-236, discusses the pentagram in relation to a variety of topics, including the Ephesia Grammata and the Daktyloi, although I would dispute his interpretation at various points. Nonetheless, it is intriguing that he arrived at these conclusions, considering that I developed this practice spontaneously and more than a year before even becoming aware of his work.

[76] Lupus, *Devotio*, pp. 60-64.

to create the "shattering reality" effect that occurred in the original dream, in order to progress the stages of the moon (connected to both Antinous and to Artemis and Hekate), so to speak. I have also performed this ritual using a wand, with one hand, in a similar fashion. If you choose to adopt a practice similar to this, you might consider adapting it to your own preferences, under the guidance of your own deities and holy powers, to maximize its connection to and relevance for your own personal spiritual technologies.

Below, I give the text of the "Dream Spell of Antinous" that was used at the Antinoan Dream Incubation Ritual at PantheaCon 2013. The section containing the Ephesia Grammata toward the end is done using the gestures learned in the dream just discussed; feel free to adapt it to your own purposes.

Dream Spell of Antinous

Come to me, Antinous, from your earthly
    dwelling-places,
upon the shores of the Nile where Thoth is,
from the city of oracle-giving Bes,
ANOUTH ANOUTH,
and from the province of Bithynia rich in pine
    trees,
the place of dream-giving goddesses,
AKTIOPHIS MARZOUNE MENE MENE,
come to me in your beautiful form,
skin like honey-colored pentelic marble
with gentle eyes and inviting lips,
AIOOE AIOOE AIOOE,
and during my nights of sleep and dreams
do not let hostile *daimones* bring me trouble,
but instead watch guard over me in your hero's
    form,
in a black breastplate dark like coal soot,
with an adamantine helmet covering your head—
the sweat from your brow the smell of storax,
the dust from your hair the scent of burnt cedars,

ACHELEJ ACHELEJ ACHELEJ,[77]
and may the light from your thyrsus like a beacon
show through every darkness of fear
and may your form come to me and speak with
    me.
By the names that give power in Ephesus,
ASKION   KATASKION   LIX   TETRAX
    DAMNAMANEUS AISIA
ASKION   KATASKION   LIX   TETRAX
    DAMNAMANEUS AISIA
ASKION   KATASKION   LIX   TETRAX
    DAMNAMANEUS AISIA
may I be protected in my dream journey
and may my soul be illuminated and improved.
ANTINOE ACHELEJ AZOMENOI AIOEEOU
MASKELLI MASKELLO ANOUTH ANOUTH

---

[77] This is a divine name that was revealed in a dream that I had in the early part of 2010; see Lupus, *Devotio*, p. 86. Further investigation has revealed that this is the Serbo-Croatian rendering (in Romanized script) of the name of the hero Achilleus; one of the major inscriptions recording Antinous as a hero, connected to Hadrian and Aelius Caesar, was found in Socanica, now in Serbia, and Antinous was compared to Achilleus by Arrian of Nikomedia in one of his writings to Hadrian—see Lupus, *Devotio*, pp. 289, 382-384.

*MELIOUCHOS   ANTINOOS   ANTINOUS
    ANTINOE*
IAOAI IAOAI IAOAI
And may what passes before the eyes of my mind
be preserved by Mnemosyne when the light of
	Eos comes.

* * * * *

Androkydes the Pythagorean suggests, in the excerpt of his lost work quoted by Clement of Alexandria, that *DAMNAMENEUS* signifies "the sun." The use of the sun or a solar deity's name as a protective device, including within the context of a dream vision, has an intriguing history that includes the fifth-century CE *Confessio* of St. Patrick, the well-known patron saint of Ireland. Though he is best known for a protective *lorica* spell/prayer that dates from the medieval period, and several centuries after his purported life,[78] the protective quality of the

---

[78] John Carey, *King of Mysteries: Early Irish Religious Writings* (Dublin: Four Courts Press, 2000), pp. 127-135.

Greek name of the solar god, Helios, occurs as the device via which Patrick is able to overcome Satan crushing him with a rock in a dream.[79] Though the sun itself has christological implications within the realm of Christian religiosity (e.g. Jesus as the "Sun of Justice"), there is some question as to whether or not Patrick was what we might think of as an "orthodox" Christian in every respect, or whether he may have been a syncretic solar monotheist,[80] not unlike many other people in late antiquity.

Whatever the truth on this matter might be, and whether or not *DAMNAMENEUS* truly does signify "the sun," what becomes clear in examining some ancient texts is that, at very least, *DAMNAMENEUS* is considered a divine being of some description. That, and the possibility that the other Ephesia Grammata, as-a-

---

[79] Whitley Stokes (ed.), *The Tripartite Life of St. Patrick, with other documents relating to that Saint*, 2 vols. (London: Her Majesty's Stationery Office, 1887), Vol. 2, p. 363.

[80] Timothy E. Powell, "Christianity or Solar Monotheism: The Early Religious Beliefs of St. Patrick," *The Journal of Ecclesiastical History* 43.4 (1991), pp. 531-540.

whole or separately, are divine beings, or can assist one in connecting to divine beings, is the subject of the next chapter.

AISIA:
"True Voice/Word"

The Ephesia Grammata as Divine Grammatical Beings

IN common with many *voces magicae*, the Ephesia Grammata may have been seen as the "secret" names of, or connected to, particular deities.[81] However, there is also some evidence that they may have been seen as some form of divine being in themselves as well.[82] John G. Gager writes, "already on the early Hellenistic amulet from Crete, the originally impersonal *ephesia grammata* are addressed as powers in their own right: they have become the names of supernatural entities,

---

[81] Fritz Graf, "Prayer in Magical and Religious Ritual," in Christopher A. Faraone and Dirk Obbink (eds.), *Magika Hiera: Ancient Greek Magic & Religion* (Oxford and New York: Oxford University Press, 1991), pp. 188-213 at 191-192.

[82] Clinton E. Arnold, *Ephesians: Power and Magic, The Concept of Power in Ephesians in Light of its Historical Setting* (Cambridge: Cambridge University Press, 1989), p. 16.

just as the later *voces mysticae* come to function as the secret and powerful names of the gods invoked in the spells."[83] Perhaps it is worth quoting one older translation of the Phalasarna tablet text in question in full, since the translation given in an earlier chapter might obscure this particular dimension of it.

> Hear ye, malicious pack that infesteth the Aethalian country,
> Forth from our homes, I say, away to your own dwelling places.
> Zeus, the averter of evil, and Heracles, sacker of cities,
> Healer, I call upon thee, on Victory, and on Apollo.
> Hear ye; the Lix of Tetrag the leaping flock now is bringing.
> Epaphos, Epaphos, Epaphos, flee; thou she-wolf, flee also;
> Dog, and thou Thieving Demon, thy fellow insatiate, together

---

[83] John G. Gager, *Curse Tablets and Binding Spells from the Ancient World* (Oxford and New York: Oxford University Press, 1992), p. 7.

Flee ye away, infuriate raging, each to his dwelling.
Keep off from the banquet the two greedy hell-hounds, O Aski Kataski.
Aski Kataski, Aisia Lix, at milking time firmly
Drive ye the wooly flock home from the meadow. Thy name is Tetrag,
But thou, O Wind, hast the name of Swift, a guerdon of Zeus.
Happily he who knows binding magic may pass down the highway,
Shorn of his senses the silent, traversing the spirit-thronged highway.

...

Damnameneu, do thou tame by force the wickedly stubborn,
Whoso may harm me and those who some charm would cast o'er me to bind me;

...

Whoso with ointments of magic would hurt me, to him be no refuge
By ways whether trodden or trackless: to

Earth, the All-spoiler, I doom him. [84]

It certainly appears that several of the Ephesia Grammata, if not all of them mentioned here, are being referred to as if they are personal beings who can respond to prayers. There is further evidence for this as well in what may be for some a rather unexpected set of sources.

The Judeo-Christian compendium of demonological lore, *The Testament of Solomon*, dating from the third or fourth century CE, has a mention at one stage of a pair of the Ephesia Grammata in a role quite similar to that which occurs in the Cretan tablet just examined: Lix Tetrax, who is treated as a demon of storms.[85] Indeed, of all the various Ephesia Grammata, Tetrax (in various other forms) or Lix Tetrax

---

[84] Chester C. McCown, "The Ephesia Grammata in Popular Belief," *Transactions and Proceedings of the American Philological Association* 54 (1923), pp. 128-140 at 133-134.

[85] McCown, pp. 135-139; *The Testament of Solomon, edited from Manuscripts at Mount Athos, Bologna, Holkham Hall, Jerusalem, London, Milan, Paris and Vienna* (Leipzig: J. C. Hinrichs'sche Buchhandlung, 1922), p. 29 (VII.4).

seems to be regarded quite often as a powerful being of some sort.[86]

In other Jewish magical contexts, there are hints that perhaps *ASKI KATASKI* was also seen as a divine being of some sort, since speaking those names in the form "*'SKY WBWSKY*" was prohibited.[87] However, another of the Ephesia Grammata appears as part of the invocation in a Jewish spell: *DAMNAMENEUS*. It was found in the Cairo Genizah,[88] and takes the form of a diminishing magical triangle, as follows:

---

[86] Alberto Bernabé, "The *Ephesia Grammata*: Genesis of a Magical Formula," in Christopher A. Faraone and Dirk Obbink (eds.), *The Getty Hexameters: Poetry, Magic, and Mystery in Ancient Selinous* (Oxford and New York: Oxford University Press, 2013), pp. 71-95 at 87-88, 95.

[87] Gideon Bohak, *Ancient Jewish Magic: A History* (Cambridge: Cambridge University Press, 2008), p. 387.

[88] *Genizot*, from the Hebrew root meaning "to hide away," are temporary storage rooms in synagogues used to keep worn-out religious writings, as well as secular writings, before their proper disposal by burial, because any document containing the name of the Hebrew deity cannot be destroyed or discarded carelessly.

texts of *PGM* II,[93] III,[94] and IV (the Great Magical Papyrus of Paris),[95] as well as elsewhere.

However, *DAMNAMENEUS* is probably best known as one of the names of the Idaean Daktyls.[96] The Daktyloi were also closely identified or sometimes confused with the Chalybes, Telchines, Kabiri, Korybantes, and Kouretes, and indeed Damneus (being essentially equivalent to Damnameneus) is given as the name of one of the Kouretes as well.[97] Pherekydes of

---

[93] Betz, *Greek Magical Papyri*, p. 17 (II.163).
[94] Betz, *Greek Magical Papyri*, pp. 20 (III.80), 21 (III.100), 30 (III.443), 32 (III.511).
[95] Betz, *Greek Magical Papyri*, p. 90 (IV.2772, 2780).
[96] Bernabé, p. 88; Jake Stratton-Kent, *Geosophia: The Argo of Magic*, 2 Volumes (Dover: Scarlet Imprint, 2010), Vol. 2, pp. 56-58; Johan August Alm, *Tartaros: On the Orphic and Pythagorean Underworld, and the Pythagorean Pentagram* (Hercules, CA: Three Hands Press, 2013), pp. 140-151.
[97] Stratton-Kent, Vol. 1, pp. 227-233. For an excellent collection of the ancient Greek and Roman sources, in translation, on the Kouretes and Daktyloi, see Aaron J. Atsma, "Daktyloi & Kouretes," *The Theoi Project* (2000-2011), http://www.theoi.com/Georgikos/Kouretes.html . Indeed, it was in this particular connection and context, of the Daktyloi, Kouretes, and others' involvement in magic and metalwork, that I first engaged with the Ephesia Grammata in a poem: P. Sufenas Virius Lupus, "The Golden Net," in Rebecca Buchanan (ed.), *Harnessing*

Syros wrote a lost treatise (now known only in fragments) on the Daktyloi.[98] Clement of Alexandria's *Stromateis* also includes the statement that the Daktyloi invented the Ephesia Grammata.[99]

Fritz Graf and Sarah Iles Johnston point out that the Daktyloi were said to have been connected to Orpheus as well, according to Diodorus of Sicily:

> The Idaean Dactyls were born in the region of Mt. Ida in Phrygia; they migrated with Mygdon to Europe. Being *goetes*, they spent their time with spells (*epoidai*), initiations and mystery cults.

Fire: A Devotional Anthology in Honor of Hephaestus (Asheville, NC: Bibliotheca Alexandrina, 2013), pp. 175-182 at 177.

[98] Sandra Blakely, "Pherekydes' *Daktyloi*: Ritual, Technology, and the Presocratic Perspective," *Kernos* 20 (2007), http://kernos.revues.org/161.

[99] Gulielmi Dindorfii, *Clementis Alexandrini Opera*, Vol. 2 (Oxford: Clarendon Press, 1869), p. 60 (I.15.73); Radcliffe G. Edmonds III, "The *Ephesia Grammata*: *Logos Orphaïkos* or Apolline *Alexima Pharmaka*?" in Christopher A. Faraone and Dirk Obbink (eds.), *The Getty Hexameters: Poetry, Magic, and Mystery in Ancient Selinous* (Oxford and New York: Oxford University Press, 2013), pp. 97-106 at 103; Blakely §18; McCown, "Ephesia Grammata," p. 129.

> When they were living about the island of Samothrace, they quite frightened the indigenous inhabitants with all these things. At this time also, Orpheus became their student, although his different nature had first driven him to poetry and music; and it was he who first brought initiations and mystery cults to the Greeks.[100]

Recall that in *PGM* VII, the phrase "Orphic formula" is used in reference to the Ephesia Grammata, and that likewise in *PGM* LXX, the initiatory *katabasis* sequence that seems to be a part of the spell indicates time spent in the cave of the Daktyloi.[101] While Radcliffe G. Edmonds thinks that all connection to Orphic tradition with the Ephesia Grammata can be discounted, and that the connection to the Daktyloi is likewise simply because the hexameters from

---

[100] Fritz Graf and Sarah Iles Johnston, *Ritual Texts for the Afterlife: Orpheus and the Bacchic Gold Tablets* (London and New York: Routledge, 2007), p. 170.
[101] Betz, *Greek Magical Papyri*, pp. 129-130 (VII.429-458), 297-298 (LXX.4-25).

which the Ephesia Grammata developed were dactylic, at the same time, the appeal of these mythic narratives to the overall development of the Ephesia Grammata and its usage, and the support for their existence as supernatural or divine beings of some sort, cannot be so easily discounted.

A final possibility of the connections of the Ephesia Grammata to divine beings of some nature in the ancient world must be discussed before moving into more practical and modern dimensions of the discussion. It has been pointed out to me[102] that one of the *PGM* formulae for invoking the "Headless God"[103] contains an interesting phrase, specifically in *PGM* V.96-172's "Stele of Jeu the Hieroglyphist." After the words which are spoken (the majority of the text of this spell), the following instructions are given: "*Preparation for the foregoing ritual*: Write the formula on a new sheet of paper, and after extending it from one of your temples to the

---

[102] For this insight, I am entirely indebted to Jeremy Glick.
[103] On this entity, see Betz, *Greek Magical Papyri*, p. 335.

other, read the **six names**, while you face north [emphasis mine]..."[104] The spoken spell before this contains various non-Ephesia Grammata *voces magicae*, but none of them are a sequence of six. Could this be another reference to the Ephesia Grammata? As the Headless God is often connected to or thought synonymous with Osiris, and the *PGM* VII formula which calls the Ephesia Grammata "Orphic" mainly deals with Osiris, perhaps this is possible.

Thus, ample precedent exists to consider the possibility that, at very least, *LIX TETRAX* and *DAMNAMENEUS* were considered, respectively, a *daimon* of storms and one of the Daktyloi or Kouretes. However, what I am suggesting in this chapter is that all of the canonical Ephesia Grammata (including the seventh, *ENDASION*) might be what we could refer to as "divine grammatical beings." This might be though of as a variety of *daimon*, a classification of divine being most often considered in the ancient world as existing on a continuum somewhere between

---

[104] Betz, *Greek Magical Papyri*, p. 103 (V.160).

deities and deified mortals.[105] In Roman terms, we might think of them as *numina*,[106] which could have developed from deified abstractions, as the various Roman divinized virtues did (e.g. Pietas, Honos, Disciplina, etc.).

When dealing with magical texts, it is important to realize that words, and even individual letters and sounds, are magical in themselves, as both symbols and sounds,[107] and thus the Ephesia Grammata are particularly potent and multi-purpose in this regard. Just as any letter-based system of magic or sortilege-based divination—from Yoruba Ifa to Norse runes to Irish ogam to Hebrew lots, or even more complex text-based systems like the Homeric oracles—can be thought of as a kind of "programming language" for a particular culture or system of spirituality, so too might the Ephesia Grammata be

---

[105] For further information on this, see Marcus Collisson, *Michael Psellus on the Operation of Daemons*, introduced by Stephen Skinner (Singapore: Golden Hoard Press, 2010).
[106] Lesley Adkins and Roy A. Adkins, *Dictionary of Roman Religion* (New York: Facts on File, 1996), p. 165 *s.v. numen*.
[107] Joscelyn Godwin, *The Mystery of the Seven Vowels in Theory and Practice* (Grand Rapids: Phanes Press, 1991).

envisioned in this fashion, connecting to Graeco-Egyptian magic, to Orphic practice, to Pythagoreanism, to Thracian religion, or to the specific cultic spheres of the Daktyloi and Kouretes, Apollon, Hekate, and Artemis of Ephesus in particular.

The sacred syllables in the mantras of Hindu tradition, likewise, connect the speaker of those syllables to the deities concerned. In some cases, mantras or the names of deities in Hinduism (especially Ram) can become independent divine powers in themselves; and this is not unprecedented in other polytheistic religio-cultural spiritual systems either. Indeed, no matter what, this seems to be what occurred in antiquity with the Ephesia Grammata. However one might categorize them theologically, the Ephesia Grammata are words and names of power, whether entities in themselves or as channels of connection to greater divine beings.

Since 2011, I have been working with a new group of deities known as the Tetrad++ Group;

originally, there were four,[108] but as of late 2012 and early 2013, there have been six. Ever since October of 2011, however, the original four of the Tetrad++ Group's symbol, as revealed by Anubis in an oracular session, has been a six-pointed star. This confused me for a while, and so in the other spaces of the symbol where there was not yet a Tetrad++ Group member represented, instead the letters for Set and Lucius Marius Vitalis (as the final "fathers" in their mythological origin story) were located. Once there are six members of the group, giving them each one of the points seemed logical.

Rather than taking the "implied" and divinatory meanings of the Ephesia Grammata as the guide to which patterns might fit the Tetrad++ Group, I've generally taken their meanings more literally, and have ended up with the following associations.

---

[108] P. Sufenas Virius Lupus, *All-Soul, All-Body, All-Love, All-Power: A TransMythology* (Anacortes: The Red Lotus Library, 2012).

ASKION: Panpsyche
KATASKION: Panprosdexia
LIX: Panhyle
TETRAX: Pancrates
DAMNAMENEUS: Paneros
AISIA: Paneris

While this is not at all their canonical order of birth or emergence, it has its own internal logic. Standing between Panpsyche (male-to-female trans*) and Panhyle (female-to-male trans*) is Panprosdexia (non-gendered): the two most strongly conventionally gendered (even though they're trans*!) members of the group have a non-gendered being between them. And both Pancrates (pangendered) and Paneris (gender-fluid) are, in certain respects, "both" genders (even though there are more than two), whereas Paneros (metagendered) is "another."

Further, more can be said on each of the Tetrad++ Group's connections to each of the Ephesia Grammata.

Panpsyche as connected to *ASKION* is therefore

"shadowless," because she represents in certain people's minds the ultimate "shadow" side of the entire construct of kyriarchal society: that someone assigned male at birth might not be male, and thus by her very existence she undermines the entire system. She is the shadow herself, and thus has no shadow, and is a being of almost perfect light and perfect soul with little to no shadow issues.

Panprosdexia connected to Kataskion is "shadowy," and if anything emerged in the work writing "The Sixth,"[109] it was that Panprosdexia is the one born in shadow, fostered in shadow (as, literally, her foster-mother Scáthach's name also means "shadowy"!), and the least afraid of venturing into the shadows to do their work.

Panhyle connected to *LIX* makes sense, because the letter is usually interpreted as meaning "earth," and Panhyle is the most earthy of the Tetrad++ Group. He is grounded, he is very

---

[109] The poem on Panprosdexia's birth, which I hope to publish in the near future.

straight-forward, he is decisive and secure, and also often relatively silent and soft-spoken. Not unlike the earth itself, Panhyle's existence and his gender status *simply is*, and that's that. Panhyle's sacred animal is the bull, which has horns, not unlike the goat, the latter of which may be the original form or inspiration of this particular Ephesia Grammata.

Pancrates' connection to *TETRAX* is because sie was the fourth member of the group to emerge; but also, *TETRAX* is interpreted to mean "the four seasons" and thus "time," and thus "transformation" and change may also be implied. Pancrates is pangendered, which means that sie contains all of the possible genders in hirself, and thus is kind of a rebus of "every season" on a physical and metaphysical level.

Paneros' connection to *DAMNAMENEUS* occurs because the letter's name is understood to mean "the sun." The colors gold and yellow are connected to Paneros, and because Paneros is concerned with 100% universal love, friendship, and sexuality, that is a rather "warm" thing which many people may wish to gather under and worship (and, indeed, at the Tetrad++ ritual at PantheaCon in 2013, a huge number of people declared as much in relation to Paneros!). In the Tetrad++'s mythic cycle, Paneros is able to command Zeus, Poseidon, and Hades, and frees Eros himself from chains he did not even realize bound him, and thus the etymological meaning behind *DAMNAMENEUS* as "conqueror" or "dominator" is also appropriate.

But, further, the upward-pointing triangle of the hexangular symbol has at its top point Panprosdexia, which is "shadowy," but Panprosdexia is the member of the group most dedicated to bringing everyone "back to the light"; thus, the downward-pointing triangle should have at its lowest point the most opposite member, which would be Paneros as "the sun." Paneros brought eir light down to some of the lowest levels of the underworld at the River Styx, so the orientation of these two within the hexangular structure is mythologically sound.

And, finally, Paneris connected to *AISIA* is

sensible because it can mean (in extension) "*logos*." Why does that make sense? In "The Marriage of Paneros,"[110] Paneris confronts Paneros with the limits and limitations of thought. Just as Panpsyche is "shadowless" because she questions and undermines the whole system, Paneris likewise is "*logos*" because in his/her transformations and constantly running the gamut of the binary gender system, she/he questions its existence and its limits and its logic, and uses those limits and that ordering principle in order to do so.

In a similar fashion, one could use the meanings of the Ephesia Grammata given by Androkydes or Hesychius to correlate these qualities and associations with deities that you might already be working with, no matter what culture they originate from—though Mediterranean cultures are probably the most sensible and familiar for these purposes. As ever, one should first and foremost consult not only the deities one is

---

[110] The poem on Paneris' birth, which I hope to publish in the near future.

engaged with themselves, but one might also entreat the Ephesia Grammata as divine grammatical beings as well for their assistance in this process.

I would suggest the following connections for the six letters of the Ephesia Grammata and some of the most important deities related to Orphic, as well as general Greek and Egyptian, as well as my own Antinous-specific, polytheistic practice:

ASKION—Hades, Nyx, Erebos, Thanatos, Ereshkigal, Nergal
KATASKION—Persephone, Melinoe, Osiris, Set, Bendis, Kotys
LIX—Demeter, Gaia, Rhea, Cybele, Pan, Hathor
TETRAX—Selene, Artemis, Dionysos, Bes, Anubis, Chnoubis
DAMNAMENEUS—Apollon, Helios, Zeus, Herakles, Antinous, Sabazios
AISIA—Hermes, Hekate, Artemis, Isis, Thoth, Glykon

ENDASION:
"Kindling Hairy Distributors (?!?)"

The Ephesia Grammata as Divinatory System

THE accounts in a previous chapter on the Ephesia Grammata's usage as amulets—found in the *Suda*, Eustathius, and Photius—which indicated that an Ephesian wrestler carried the letters on his person inscribed on a knucklebone, already hints at the possible usage of the Ephesia Grammata for divinatory purposes. Knucklebones was a common Greek game, but they were also used in the practice of astragalomancy, or divination based on how a group of knucklebones fell, as if the bones were dice.[111] However, the Ephesia Grammata—

---

[111] See the recent system of astragalomancy, based on inscriptions from various ancient temples, in Kostas Derveni, *Oracle Bones Divination: The Greek I Ching* (Rochester, VT and Toronto: Destiny Books, 2014).

generally six in number—do not necessarily align easily on knucklebones, since these tend to have four workable faces in terms of their casting for divinatory purposes (though there are possibilities for their usage in this manner—on which, see further below). However, one must take account of other realities about the matter of divinatory usage before engaging in this practice.

To state it plainly, there is no currently known evidence of the Ephesia Grammata being used as a system of divination in the ancient world, by anyone, at any period of time.[112] Why, therefore, spend a whole chapter of the present book on the subject? The answer is somewhat long and rambling, but hopefully worth your attention.

When I started working with the Ephesia Grammata as a divinatory system several years ago, I had recalled reading that they were used as

---

[112] Sarah Iles Johnston, *Ancient Greek Divination* (Malden, Oxford, and Chichester: Wiley-Blackwell, 2008), a thorough and highly acclaimed academic work, contains no references to the Ephesia Grammata being employed for the purposes of divination.

such, but could not recall where I had heard or read this. After doing as much research as possible on the matter and finding nothing, and searching my notes from several different academic and esoteric conferences, I simply resolved to continue using them for divination, and I hoped to remember the reference or re-encounter them at some future point. This did not occur until early February of 2014, when I had occasion to look up the madrona[113] tree in Randy Conner, David Hatfield Sparks and Mariya Sparks' *Cassell's Encyclopedia of Queer Myth, Symbol and Spirit*. It happens that this entry is a few pages before that for the Megabyzoi, which I passed as I was about to read the information on the tree. Having not read about the Megabyzoi for many years at that point, I reviewed the entry on this gender-variant priesthood of Artemis of Ephesus. Included in it was the following statement:

---

[113] This is an Oregon-Washington idiolect for the tree which, elsewhere, is spelled "madrone."

> The *megabyzoi* were best known, however, for their ability to divine the future by way of the Ephesian Letters. Roughly equivalent to Teutonic runes, the letters, made of wood and painted gold, were carried in pouches that hung from the waist. They were employed not only as a divinatory tool but were also believed to function as amulets or talismans, protecting the wearer from harm.[114]

Not having thought to look previously in the encyclopedia for information on the Ephesia Grammata, I then consulted that cross-referenced entry.

> The *megabyzoi*, the transgendered male priest/esse/s of the Greco-Roman goddess Artemis/Diana, were best known for their ability to divine the

---

[114] Randy P. Conner, David Hatfield Sparks and Mariya Sparks, *Cassell's Encyclopedia of Queer Myth, Symbol and Spirit: Covering Gay, Lesbian, Bisexual and Transgender Lore* (London and New York: Cassell, 1997), p. 230 *s.v.* Megabyzos.

> future by way of the Ephesian Letters. The poet Anaxilas refers to their "carrying in sewn leather bags / The Ephesian letters of gold omen." Roughly equivalent to Teutonic runes, the letters, made of wood and painted gold, were carried in pouches that hung from the waist. The letters were six in number and named *aschion, chataschion, lix* (or *aix*), *tatras, damsmeneus*, and *asia*; they may have referred to darkness, light, earth (or water), the seasons of the year, the sun, and truth.[115]

While I noted the odd form of the traditional six letters given, I was frustrated that no reference for the information on their use as divinatory equipment was listed (indeed, this is one of the greatest frustrations of using this particular encyclopedic source in general!). However, I recalled that there was a section on the Megabyzoi in Conner's other book, *Blossom of Bone*. The paragraph therein written on this

---

[115] Conner, Sparks, and Sparks, p. 131 *s.v.* Ephesian Letters.

matter is a near duplicate of the two sections given above, leaving out the names of the letters and varying slightly in their definitions of them.[116] However, a reference was given there,[117] to Edward Falkener's book, *Ephesus, and the Temple of Diana*. The relevant passage, quoted here in full, reads:

> Among the superstitions most connected with Ephesus, are what were called the "Ephesian Letters," which were these:— ασκιον, κατασκιον, λιξ, τετραξ, δαμναμενευς, and αισια. "The Ephesian Letters were (said to be) charms, with which, if anyone were furnished, he became invincible. Thus a wrestler wearing them, (or according to the *Adag. Diog.* iv. 78, uttering them) became a victor thirty times. But if they were discovered, or taken away by his adversary, he was immediately conquered." Croesus

---

[116] Randy P. Conner, *Blossom of Bone: Reclaiming the Connections Between Homoeroticism and the Sacred* (New York: HarperCollins Publishers, 1993), p. 96.

[117] Conner, p. 315 note 56.

is said to have escaped being burned alive, by having pronounced them on the pyre; and magicians were believed to exorcise demoniacs and those possessed of evil spirits, by causing them to recite to themselves these famous letters. Androcydes, the Pythagorean philosopher, tells us they were held in much estimation by the vulgar: and in the Metrical Proverbs, (No. 50,) we learn that they were carried in sewn leather bags; both which testimonies are confirmed by a passage in Athenaeus, containing a fragment of Anaxilas:—

"The skin anointed with golden ointment;
Effeminately dressed in soft robes
And delicate slippers—
Chewing onions; munching cheese;
Eating raw eggs; sucking shell-fish;
Quaffing goblets of rich Chian;
And carrying in sewn leather bags
The Ephesian letters of good omen."

But to investigate these letters more

closely. Clemens of Alexandria thus interprets them:

ασκιον, *darkness*.

κατασκιον, *light*, (as producing darkness.)

λιξ, *earth*, (according to its original signification.)

τετραξ, *the year*, (as being formed of the *four* seasons.)

δαμναμενευς, the sun, (because it *governs*.)

αισια, *truth*.

In place of Λιξ, Hesycliius writes Αιξ, and from the resemblance of the words it is possible that one may have been written for the other; but considering their sense, (Αιξ being put for *water*) it is probable that both these words were included in the number. Thus we shall have *light* and *darkness*; *earth* and *water*; the *sun* and the *year*; and the whole governed by *truth*. If we consider Diana as the personification of *nature*, we cannot fail to perceive that these words may have a mystical reference to the character of the goddess. Androcydes tells us, they were the symbols of divine things. Creuzer is of opinion that the sun, mentioned above, is an evidence of derivation from the fire-worship of Persia; but this does not appear borne out, neither indeed is it plausible. According to Eustathius, spells were engraved on the feet, girdle, and crown, of the statue of Diana: these might possibly have been the Ephesian Letters, or some such charm, or they might have been similar to the inscription on the foot of the statue of Neith or Minerva at Sais: "I am everything that has been, that is, and that shall be; and no mortal has ever yet been able to withdraw my veil. The fruit which I have brought forth the sun."[118]

Certainly, much of our knowledge and the translations of sources available since the mid-1800s when Falkener was writing have improved dramatically, and opinions on a variety of matters

---

[118] Edward Falkener, *Ephesus, and the Temple of Diana* (London: Day & Son, 1862), pp. 144-146.

have advanced to such a degree that his treatment—while thorough in its overall brevity—seems rather naïve now, in several particular respects. Nonetheless, there is nothing in this passage, nor any other nearby in Falkener's volume, about the use of the Ephesia Grammata for divination by the Megabyzoi. Elsewhere in the volume, Falkener discusses a priest of Artemis of Ephesus who was called Megabyzos, and after doing so, has the following to say:

> The title of Megabyzus, as it is generally written, appears to have been originally a proper name, and to have become a title of honour in consequence of Darius observing of one of his generals who was so called:—"I would rather have as many Megabyzi as there are seeds in a pomegranate, than see Greece under my power." The name might also derive importance from its first particle. Herodotus makes mention of two, if not three, of this name. A Megabyzus was one of the confederates against Smerdis Magus. His son Zopyrus had a son of the same name, Megabyzus,

who was employed as a general in the time of Xerxes. But the general of this name who is best known was contemporary, if not identical, with Megabyzus the confederate against Smerdis Magus. Again, it is possible that a priest of this name happened once to be appointed, and the Ephesians, in order to please the Persian monarchs, caused the name to be hereditary, in the same manner that titles of kings were often so. Xenophon, and Pliny, and Diogenes Laertius, refer to the priests under this name.[119]

Thus, apart from Anaxilas' fragment, as quoted in Athenaeus and discussed in a previous chapter above in its various translations, there is little to go on in terms of the Megabyzoi being at all gender-variant,[120] and even less to indicate that

---

[119] Falkener, pp. 330-331.
[120] While this is a much larger topic than can be dealt with at present, there is more reliable information on this topic in Axel W. Persson, *The Religion of Greece in Prehistoric Times* (Berkeley and Los Angeles: The University of California Press, 1942), p. 146; Jan M. Bremmer, "Priestly Personnel of the Ephesian Artemision:

the Ephesia Grammata were used for divination. This would not be the first time, however, that information in Conner, Sparks, and Sparks has created a myth of its own that can have relevance, though, and is certainly not the first time such a thing has occurred in my own life, even.[121]

Thus, despite there being no definite evidence that indicates the Ephesia Grammata were used as a tool for divination in the past, that does not preclude their usage for divination now and in the future.

* * * * *

As a basis for the divinatory meanings of the Ephesia Grammata, I have been using the passage from Clement of Alexandria, giving the symbolic

---

Anatolian, Persian, Greek, and Roman Aspects" (2008), pp. 1-21 at 1-7, available at http://theoi.eldoc.ub.rug.nl/FILES/root/2008/Priestly/Bremmer-Priests.pdf .

[121] See P. Sufenas Virius Lupus, "Homoeroticism and Hephaistos: A Modern 'Myth'," in Rebecca Buchanan (ed.), *Harnessing Fire: A Devotional Anthology in Honor of Hephaestus* (Asheville, NC: Bibliotheca Alexandrina, 2013), pp. 163-172.

interpretation of them from Androkydes the Pythagorean. To review that passage:

> *askion* signifies 'darkness,' because darkness throws no shadow (*skia*); *kataskion* signifies 'light,' since it casts shadow with its light (*katagauzei*); *lix* is an old word meaning 'the earth'; *tetrax* means the 'year,' because of the (four) seasons; *damnameneus* means the Sun, which is overpowering (*damazon*); the *aisia* means 'the true voice.' The allegory intimates that the divine things have been arranged in due order, for example, darkness in relation to light, sun to create the year, and the earth to make possible every sort of natural coming-into-being.[122]

---

[122] Richard Gordon, "Imagining Greek and Roman Magic," in Valerie Flint, Richard Gordon, Georg Luck, and Daniel Ogden, *Witchcraft and Magic in Europe, Volume 2: Ancient Greece and Rome* (London: The Athlone Press, 1999), pp. 159-275 at 239; Daniel Ogden (ed.), *Magic, Witchcraft, and Ghosts in the Greek and Roman Worlds: A Sourcebook* (Oxford and New York: Oxford University Press, 2002), p. 214 §174.

Hesychius gives a paraphrase of this material, without attribution to Androkydes, as follows:

> Ephesia Grammata: Formerly there were six, but afterwards some deceivers added others. They say that these are the names of the first ones: *askion, kataskion, lix, tetrax, damnameneus, aision*. It is clear that *askion* is darkness, *kataskion* is light, *lix* is earth, *tetrax* is the year, *damnameneus* is the sun, and *aision* is truth. Therefore these things are holy and sacred.[123]

As has been the practice in the present volume, thus, we can generally translate the meanings of the six canonical Ephesia Grammata as follows:

***ASKION*: "shadowless"** (or "darkness")
***KATASKION*: "shadowy"** (or "light")
***LIX*: "earth"**

---

[123] Radcliffe G. Edmonds III, "The *Ephesia Grammata*: *Logos Orphaïkos* or Apolline *Alexima Pharmaka*?" in Christopher A. Faraone and Dirk Obbink (eds.), *The Getty Hexameters: Poetry, Magic, and Mystery in Ancient Selinous* (Oxford and New York: Oxford University Press, 2013), pp. 97-106 at 98 note 2.

TETRAX: **"seasons"** (or "the year")
DAMNAMENEUS: **"sun"**
AISIA: **"voice/word"** (or "truth")

While one could then use Androkydes' allegory even further in interpreting which of the six letters emerges in a cosmological sense, the easiest and most efficient way to use the Ephesia Grammata—at least in my experience—is as answers to binary "yes/no" questions.

The use of the Ephesia Grammata in this fashion first requires phrasing a question as specifically as possible. Generally, this should include asking "do the gods want" or "does [the deity ___] want," etc., rather than just "should I/shouldn't I" sorts of questions. If the thoughts or opinions of a particular deity or divine being are not sought on a question, then what might be occurring is that the Ephesia Grammata themselves as divine grammatical beings may be answering the question. This, in itself, is not a bad thing, as long as it is recognized as such. One should not phrase a question generally, and then take the answer to be one's patron deity or some other divine being answering it unless the question was asked specifically in that fashion. This is one of the factors which makes personal use of divination difficult for those who are not accustomed to it, and can be a potential pitfall when one is using the Ephesia Grammata—and I say this from extensive personal experience, and months of having to refine my technique in this regard!

Though questions should be asked so as to solicit a "yes/no" answer, the fact is that this system, with its six (or seven) letters, is not strictly "yes" or "no" in its potential results, and even where that more simple matter is indicated, interpretation and discernment still must be exercised to get clarity in the situational context involved. You will note that the suggested readings given below for the usual six Ephesia Grammata are not evenly divided up into three "yes" and three "no" answers, or even two "yes," two "no," and two "neutral." Rarely is anything as simply black-and-white as such a binary system might imply for some people!

***ASKION*: "shadowless/darkness"** This is perhaps one of the two most simple and straightforward of the Ephesia Grammata to interpret. As "shadowless" implies "complete darkness," then it is obviously a negative answer, and thus a simple "no."

***KATASKION*: "shadowy/light"** As anything which might be described as "shadowy," the meaning here is necessarily nebulous, cloudy, and uncertain. As a result, it can be a "soft yes," as in "there is light present" (thus favoring Hesychius' interpretation), or it can be an answer that indicates that no certain or definite response can be given at the time. When this comes up, it might be good to ask further clarifying questions, or to re-phrase one's original inquiry; if *KATASKION* results again, then take it as settled that the matter cannot be perceived with clarity at that given moment.

***LIX*: "earth"** As there is nothing in general human experience more solid than the earth itself, and no individual object that is close to humans that looms larger, this is a definite "yes" (as Christian interpretation has favored), but instead it covers a whole range of abstracts, including "reason" generally as a human faculty, "discussion/debate," "reckoning" (as in counting but also as in a hypothesis), and even "tale/story." The more literal word given in Clement of Alexandria's text attributed to Androkydes is *phone*, "voice," but also possibly "phrase" or "sound" in general, which either aurally or semantically must be perceived and interpreted or parsed. Given the connection of reason and logic to Cartesian philosophy, and the maxim "I think, therefore I am," I often interpret this letter as "yes, if you think so," with the emphasis being put on the "if YOU think so," to the degree that one's taking it as affirmative involves one's own interpretation, and thus the responsibility of the actions or opinions involved are not of the deities questioned, or of the Ephesia Grammata themselves, but of one's own self. It can just be "a noise," as one understanding of *phoné* can indicate, thus how one hears that "true voice" is entirely subjective. It can thus be taken as a "soft yes," but one with a footnote which requires qualification and further interpretation. Often, a further question, or a better question, should follow this for confirmation purposes; if it comes up again, then one is best advised to accept that the divine beings questioned are of the opinion of "if you want to, go ahead, but it's not on us if you do, so don't complain if your results aren't spectacular!" If you favor Hesychius' interpretation, instead, then simply "it's true" would be the result. If we go with the literal, original meaning suggested by Bernabé, then it could be, as *AASIA*, "disastrous, madness, folly," or *AISIA*, "favorable, auspicious."[124] Thus, the interpretive dimension of this particular letter in context comes to the fore of necessity.

Finally, **ENDASION**. While this letter is generally not found in the canonical six Ephesia Grammata, its early attestation suggests that it might be more important to some forms of the system than it might at first seem. If you choose

---

[124] Alberto Bernabé, "The *Ephesia Grammata*: Genesis of a Magical Formula," in Christopher A. Faraone and Dirk Obbink (eds.), *The Getty Hexameters: Poetry, Magic, and Mystery in Ancient Selinous* (Oxford and New York: Oxford University Press, 2013), pp. 71-95 at 90.

to include it, I would suggest the following meanings for it:

"kindle in, light" (based on the verb *endaio*)
"distribute" (also from *endaio*)
"somewhat rough/hairy" (from the adjective *endasus*)

In fact, it is the third of these that Bernabé gives as the most likely meaning for it in its original context as a rhymed pair with *AISIA!*[125] It is thus that I have given the far-from-certain, totally conjectural, and entirely provisional meaning for this letter as "kindling hairy distributors (?!?)" previously. This could signify something being "difficult" in general, especially considering the "somewhat rough/hairy" interpretation. It could also indicate that someone or something will soon enliven, enlighten, or enflame whatever the matter at hand happens to be, based on the "kindle in, light" interpretation. Or, it could indicate that a gift is going to be received or given, or that perhaps more offerings need to be

---

[125] *Ibid.*

given to the divine beings in question if this comes up as an answer to whether or not one's sacrifices in devotional ritual have been accepted, considering the "distribute" interpretation. Or, it could mean that torch-bearing, libation-pouring satyrs will soon arrive…who knows?

As mentioned in an earlier chapter above, one might consider a divinatory set of Ephesia Grammata being made by inscribing the letters (in whatever color or with whatever substance!) on wooden pieces and carrying them in a pouch; indeed, using the same set of such inscribed letters for both protective amulet purposes and for divination is the method I myself have used for the last few years. Another option would be to use a blank six-sided die (a basic cube) for the canonical six letters, and inscribe them in that fashion. While the full letters should always be used whenever possible, it may not be feasible to inscribe *DAMNAMENEUS* on a small cube, so perhaps the following two-letter abbreviations could be used:

ASKION: **AK**
KATASKION: **KA**
LIX: **ΛΞ**
TETRAX: **TΞ**
DAMNAMENEUS: **ΔM**
AISIA: **AI**

And, if one wished to use *ENDASION* as well, and perhaps used an eight-sided die (of equilateral triangles), a sensible abbreviation would be **EN**.

As an alternative for use in a die-based system and the seven letters, one could have a cubical die, and then a coin or two-sided wooden piece or chip of some sort. On opposite sides of the die, one could put *ASKION* and *KATASKION* as an opposed pair meaning "darkness" and "light" respectively; then *AISIA* and *ENDASION* as a second opposed pair meaning "auspicious" and "difficult" respectively, and on the remaining opposite sides of the cube, *LIX* and *TETRAX*, meaning "good goat" and "bad goat" respectively (!?!). On the coin or other two-sided object, one could have *DAMNAMENEUS* on the obverse, meaning "sun" and therefore everything positive, and then on the reverse side, nothing, or perhaps some other short word (e.g. *MENE*, connected in the *PGM* corpus to the moon). One would then toss the die and the coin together, with the results on the coin either intensifying the positivity of the die reading, or negating/nullifying/neutralizing it.

If one were to use a knucklebone as both an amulet (as indicated in the *Suda*, Eustathius, and Photius) and a divinatory tool inscribed with the Ephesia Grammata, then one might consider a variation of the above system, and inscribe *ASKI KATASKI* on one face, *LIX TETRAX* on the second, *AISIA ENDASION* on the third, and *DAMNAMENEUS* on the fourth. One could then cast the bone once, and to determine whether the first or the second letter is the result (in all cases except for *DAMNAMENEUS*), cast it again, with *ASKI KATASKI* and *LIX TETRAX* indicating the first word of the pair, and *AISIA ENDASION* or *DAMNAMENEUS* indicating the second. Then, use the divinatory meanings above.

Indeed, there are many ways that one could engineer to work with the Ephesia Grammata in terms of divination: your own creative imagination, the consultation of your friends and colleagues in your spiritual community, and the advice of your deities and other divine beings are the only limits on the possibilities which could be envisioned.

ΑΣΚΙΟΝ ΚΑΤΑΣΚΙΟΝ

ΛΙΞ ΤΕΤΡΑΞ

ΔΑΜΝΑΜΕΝΕΥΣ

ΑΙΣΙΑ ΕΝΔΑΣΙΟΝ

About the Author

P. Sufenas Virius Lupus is metagender, and is the founder of the Ekklesía Antínoou—a queer, Graeco-Roman-Egyptian syncretist reconstructionist polytheist group dedicated to Antinous, the deified lover of the Roman Emperor Hadrian and related divine figures—

as well as a contributing member of the Neos Alexandria group, and a practicing Celtic Reconstructionist polytheist in the *filidecht* and *gentlidecht* traditions of Ireland (with further devotions to Romano-British, Gaulish, and Welsh deities), and a devotee of several divine ancestors and land spirits in the area of western Washington state. Lupus also occasionally participates in Shinto, Buddhist, and Hindu spiritual activities.

To date, Lupus' work has appeared in the Bibliotheca Alexandrina devotional anthologies for Artemis, Hekate, Isis and Serapis, Zeus, Pan, Thoth, Persephone, the Virgin Goddesses, and the Near Eastern deities, Hermes, Hephaistos, Hera, Demeter, the Morrígan, the Muses and Graces, and the science fiction and journeys anthologies, with further forthcoming work to appear in the devotional volumes for the Dioskouroi, Athena, the cynocephalic deities, and the science fiction anthology, as well as others. Lupus' essay, fiction, and poetry have also appeared in *Datura: An Anthology of Esoteric Poeisis*, ed. Ruby Sara (Scarlet Imprint, 2010), *Spirit of Desire: Personal Explorations of Sacred Kink*, ed. Lee Harrington (Mystic Productions Press, 2010), *Etched Offerings: Voices from the Cauldron of Story*, ed. Inanna Gabriel and C. Bryan Brown (Misanthrope Press, 2011), and *Mandragora: Further Explorations in Esoteric Poeisis*, ed. Ruby Sara

(Scarlet Imprint, 2012), Tara Miller's *Rooted in the Body, Seeking the Soul* (Megalithica, 2013), and the journals and magazines *Cirle*, *Witches & Pagans*, and *Abraxas*. As you can imagine, many more pieces are in the works, and will appear in the future, if all goes well...

Lupus is also the founder of The Red Lotus Library, and has published *The Syncretisms of Antinous* (2010), *Devotio Antinoo: The Doctor's Notes, Volume One* (2011), *All-Soul, All-Body, All-Love, All-Power: A TransMythology* (2012), *A Garland for Polydeukion* (2012), and *A Serpent Path Primer* (2012) through it, with further volumes soon to be released. Lupus also published *The Phillupic Hymns* in 2008 with Bibliotheca Alexandrina.

Lupus appears yearly at PantheaCon over President's Day in San Jose, CA, and also runs public rituals in the greater Seattle area. Lupus also writes regularly on Antinous-related subjects at the Aedicula Antinoi blog (http://aediculaantinoi.wordpress.com/).

The Syncretisms of Antinous

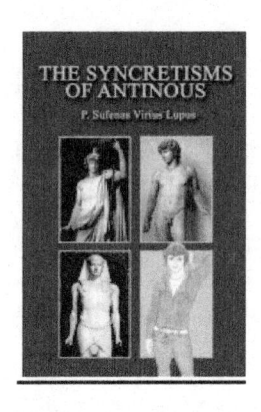

The Syncretisms of Antinous is an in-depth exploration of Antinous' relationship to other gods and heroes of the Greek, Roman, and Egyptian pantheons, both in antiquity and in later centuries. Antinous, the deified lover of the Roman Emperor Hadrian (117-138 CE), was syncretized to a large number of deities and heroes in his ancient cultus, and the process didn't stop when that cultus ended in the fifth century. Archaeologists, scholars, artists, and admirers of male beauty continued to link him to a great many figures from Greek, Roman, and Egyptian mythology. In this book, you will find out about the familiar as well as the more obscure syncretisms of Antinous, from Hermes to Herakles, Dionysos to the Dioskouroi, Apollon to Apis, Adonis to Attis, Pan to Poseidon, Achilleus to Aristaios, Endymion to Eunostos, Eros to Echmoun, and many more! You will also find resources to guide you in getting to know these syncretisms further, and ideas for devotional practices based upon them.

$20. **ISBN** **1456300458**
http://www.createspace.com/3493936

Devotio Antinoo: **The Doctor's Notes, Volume One**

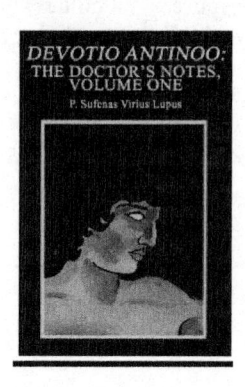

Devotio Antinoo: The Doctor's Notes, Volume One is a book that details all you'll need to start your own devotions to Antinous, including translated ancient texts and modern rituals of the Ekklesía Antínoou. The culmination of nearly ten years of research and devotion on the part of its author, *Devotio Antinoo* is presented now for the use of anyone who wishes to develop a devotional practice with Antinous, the gods with whom he was syncretized, Hadrian, other *Divi*

and many more divine figures. Learn the holy days and festivals of the year, the hymns and prayers for both regular usage and specific occasions, the ancient texts that have survived in papyrus fragments, literary excerpts, inscriptions, and ideas on different devotional activities that can be performed as well. Everything you need to practice in the tradition of the Ekklesía Antínoou is contained in this book, and much more! With an exhaustive index, *Devotio Antinoo* will be an indispensible book in the library of any syncretistic polytheist!

$35.   **ISBN**   **1468004387**
http://www.createspace.com/3735809

All-Soul, All-Body, All-Love, All-Power: A TransMythology

All-Soul, All-Body, All-Love, All-Power: A TransMythology is a new poetic myth about four transgender and gender-diverse deities, born anew for our own times and concerns, from the gods and mortals of old, with some commentary, interpretations, and history. Learn the history of the Tetrad–Panpsyche, Panhyle, Paneros, and Pancrates–for the first time in this book-length poetic narrative on their conception, birth, and histories. A trans-positive, polyamorotheist, super-syncretistic, queer extravaganza of a tale featuring Antinous, Polydeukion, and a veritable who's-who of gender-variant deity cameos from many cultures worldwide! Arising in part from a response to the transgender exclusionary events of PantheaCon 2011/2012, as well as the author's own experience as a metagender person, and a devotee of a wide variety of queer-friendly deities, this is one of the first attempts at a completely modern, trans-specific, trans-positive mythic narrative. With artwork by Nicole Hernandez, Michael Sebastian Lvx, and Jory Mickelson.

$20.   ISBN   1475025289
https://www.createspace.com/3823195

A Garland for Polydeukion

A Garland for Polydeukion is the first detailed and dedicated treatment of Polydeukion, the heroized youth who was a foster-son to Herodes Attikos, from a polytheist perspective. Learn all about Polydeukion and his fellow Trophimoi, Achilles and Memnon, as well as Herodes Attikos, his wife Appia Annia Regilla, and their other children (including Athenais, Elpinike, Regillus, and Attikos Bradua). Poetry inspired by their modern polytheist devotion is also included, as well as several essays and some fiction dealing with them in various ways.

$20. **ISBN** **147824383X**
http://www.createspace.com/3937384

A Serpent Path Primer

A Serpent Path Primer is an exploration of the Ekklesía Antínoou's theological system and spiritual methodology for mapping the syncretisms of Antinous, opening a divine window into further relationship with him and the deities and heroes to whom he is linked. Included in the volume is an in-depth examination of syncretism, both historically and in its most fruitful modern polytheist understandings, and nine Appendices.

$20. **ISBN** **1479241709**
http://www.createspace.com/3984491

Coming soon from
THE RED LOTUS LIBRARY

For the Queens of Heaven: Poems for the Goddesses A book of poetry, collecting all of the poems—of which more than a hundred have been written in 2014—to a variety of goddesses across many traditions from the span of Lupus' polytheistic life and practice of the last twenty-plus years.

Polytheist Reconstructionism as Methodology A workbook, developed for usage in the Academia Antinoi course, on how reconstructionism is best understood not as a religious path in itself, but as a methodology for use in building a spiritual practice.

Studium Antinoi: The Doctor's Notes, Volume Two Studies in theology and ethics, both new and from P. Sufenas Virius Lupus' old website, Aedicula Antinoi.

Liber Dies Antinoi An in-depth detailing of the Ekklesía Antínoou calendar and the *Sancti*, formatted for use as a "book of days."

The Triads of Antinous A gnomic text for ease in understanding theological shorthand for Antinous and within Ekklesía Antínoou practice.

COMING IN 2014 (and later)!
**For More Information, see
http://aediculaantinoi.wordpress.com/the-red-lotus-library/**

Printed in Great Britain
by Amazon